Table of Contents

Introduction

Part I: Foundations of Remote Project Management
Chapter 1. Understanding the Remote Work Landscape
  - Benefits and Challenges of Remote Work
  - Tools and Technologies for Remote Collaboration
  - Establishing a Productive Remote Work Environment

Chapter 2: Key Skills for Remote Project Managers
  - Communication and Active Listening
  - Time Management and Organization
  - Leadership and Motivation
  - Adaptability and Problem-Solving

Part II: Managing Projects in a Remote Setting
Chapter 3. Project Planning and Initiation
  - Defining Project Scope and Objectives
  - Creating a Project Charter and Plan
  - Assembling Your Virtual Team
  - Conducting Effective Kick-Off Meetings

Chapter 4: Project Execution and Monitoring
  - Assigning Tasks and Responsibilities
  - Tracking Progress and Milestones
  - Managing Project Budgets and Resources
  - Handling Project Changes and Risks

Chapter 5: Project Communication and Collaboration
  - Establishing Communication Protocols
  - Running Productive Virtual Meetings

- Using Collaboration Tools Effectively
- Providing Regular Updates and Feedback

Chapter 6: Project Closure and Evaluation
  - Conducting Project Reviews and Retrospectives
  - Documenting Lessons Learned
  - Celebrating Project Successes
  - Transitioning to New Projects

Part III: Leading and Empowering Virtual Teams
Chapter 7: Building Trust and Rapport
  - Fostering Open Communication
  - Encouraging Team Bonding and Socializing
  - Demonstrating Empathy and Emotional Intelligence
  - Leading by Example

Chapter 8: Strategies for Effective Team Collaboration
  - Defining Clear Roles and Responsibilities
  - Setting Team Goals and Expectations
  - Facilitating Brainstorming and Problem-Solving Sessions
  - Encouraging Knowledge Sharing and Peer Support

Chapter 9: Managing Team Performance and Development
  - Setting Performance Metrics and KPIs
  - Providing Regular Feedback and Coaching
  - Conducting Virtual Performance Reviews
  - Supporting Professional Development and Growth

Part IV: Mastering the Art of Remote Leadership
Chapter 10: Adapting Your Leadership Style for Remote Work
  - Understanding Different Leadership Styles

How to Become a Successful Remote Project Manager and Lead Virtual Teams

The Ultimate Guide to Managing Projects, Collaborating with Distributed Teams, and Delivering Results in a Remote Work Environment

The Fix It Guy

Copyright © 2024 by The Fix It Guy

All rights reserved. No part of this book may be reproduced in any form or by any electronic or mechanical means, including information storage and retrieval systems, without permission in writing from the publisher, except by a reviewer who may quote brief passages in a review.

- Adjusting Your Approach for Virtual Teams
- Balancing Direction and Autonomy
- Cultivating a Growth Mindset

Chapter 11: Navigating Challenges and Conflicts
- Identifying and Addressing Common Remote Work Challenges
- Resolving Conflicts and Disagreements
- Managing Underperformance and Disciplinary Issues
- Maintaining Team Morale and Engagement

Chapter 12: Promoting Work-Life Balance and Wellbeing
- Encouraging Healthy Work Habits and Boundaries
- Supporting Mental Health and Stress Management
- Recognizing Signs of Burnout and Overwork
- Modeling Self-Care and Personal Development

Conclusion
- Putting Your Skills into Practice
- Continual Learning and Improvement
- The Future of Remote Project Management

Introduction

Hey there, friend! Are you ready to unlock the incredible power of Facebook advertising and take your business to new heights? You're in the right place!

In today's digital age, Facebook has become an indispensable tool for businesses of all sizes. With over 2.8 billion monthly active users, this platform offers an unparalleled opportunity to reach your target audience, engage with potential customers, and drive meaningful results. Whether you're a small local shop or a multinational corporation, Facebook advertising has the potential to transform your marketing efforts and skyrocket your growth.

But here's the thing: simply having a Facebook page isn't enough. To truly harness the power of this platform, you need to master the art of Facebook advertising. That's where I come in! As a seasoned Facebook Ads Manager, I've helped countless businesses create effective campaigns that not only captivate their audience but also generate incredible ROI.

In this book, I'll be sharing my journey from a curious newcomer to a successful Facebook Ads Manager. Trust me, it wasn't always easy! I've made my fair share of mistakes along the way, but those experiences have taught me invaluable lessons that I can't wait to share with you. Through a combination of personal anecdotes, proven strategies, and actionable advice, I'll guide you through the process of creating, optimizing, and scaling your Facebook ad campaigns.

But this book isn't just about my story. It's about empowering you to become a master of Facebook advertising in your own right. Whether you're a business owner looking to expand your online presence, a marketer eager to add a valuable skill to your arsenal, or an aspiring Facebook Ads Manager ready to kickstart your career, this book is designed to help you achieve your goals.

So, what can you expect from this book? We'll dive deep into the fundamentals of Facebook advertising, exploring the ins and outs of the Ads Manager dashboard, defining your target audience, and crafting compelling ad copy and visuals. But we won't stop there! I'll also share advanced strategies for split testing, retargeting, and scaling your campaigns to maximize your results.

Throughout the book, you'll find real-world case studies and success stories that showcase the incredible potential of Facebook advertising. From local businesses that tripled their revenue to e-commerce stores that scaled to seven figures, these examples will inspire you to dream big and take action.

But perhaps the most valuable aspect of this book is the actionable advice and resources I'll be sharing. You'll find checklists, templates, and cheat sheets designed to help you implement what you learn and start seeing results right away. And as a special bonus, I've included a glossary of Facebook advertising terms and a list of recommended tools to help you streamline your workflow and stay ahead of the curve.

Part I
Foundations of Remote Project Management

Chapter 1
Understanding the Remote Work Landscape
Benefits and Challenges of Remote Work

The rise of remote work has revolutionized the way we think about work and collaboration. No longer bound by the confines of a traditional office, teams can now span the globe, bringing together the best and brightest minds to work on projects from anywhere with an internet connection. It's an exciting time, but navigating this new landscape can be a challenge, especially for project managers tasked with leading virtual teams.

Let's start with the good news: the benefits of remote work are numerous and significant. First and foremost, remote work offers an unparalleled level of flexibility. Without the need to commute or adhere to a strict 9-to-5 schedule, team members can work when and where they're most productive. For some, that might mean starting the day early and finishing by afternoon. For others, it might mean working in short bursts throughout the day, with breaks for exercise, errands, or family time. This flexibility can lead to increased job satisfaction, reduced stress, and a better work-life balance.

Remote work also allows companies to tap into a global talent pool. No longer limited by geographic location, you can assemble a team of the best and brightest from around the world. This diversity of perspectives and experiences can lead to more creative problem-solving and innovation. Plus, with no need for physical office space, companies can save on overhead costs and invest those resources into their people and products.

But remote work isn't all sunshine and rainbows. There are challenges that come with leading a virtual team, and it's important to be aware of them from the outset. Communication is perhaps the biggest hurdle. When you're not sharing the same physical space, it's easy for misunderstandings to occur and for important information to slip through the cracks. It's crucial to establish clear communication channels and protocols, whether that's through regular video calls, instant messaging, or project management software like Trello or Asana.

Another challenge is building trust and rapport with your team. In a traditional office setting, you have countless opportunities for casual interactions and relationship-building. You might chat with a colleague over coffee in the break room, or grab lunch with your team after a big meeting. In a remote setting, those informal moments are harder to come by. As a project manager, it's your job to be intentional about creating opportunities for connection and team-building, whether that's through virtual happy hours, team-building exercises, or just casual check-ins.

There's also the issue of work-life balance. When your home is your office, it can be tempting to work around the clock. But burnout is a real risk, and it's important to set boundaries and encourage your team to do the same. This might mean establishing clear working hours, taking regular breaks throughout the day, and making time for hobbies and self-care outside of work.

Despite these challenges, the benefits of remote work are too significant to ignore. With the right mindset, tools, and strategies, you can lead your virtual team to success and enjoy the many perks of the remote work lifestyle. In the following sections, we'll dive deeper into the specific skills and techniques you need to thrive as a remote project manager.

So, whether you're a seasoned pro or just starting out, this chapter is your foundation. By understanding the landscape of remote work - both the benefits and the challenges - you'll be better equipped to navigate the road ahead. And trust us, it's an exciting road indeed. So grab your map (or, let's be real, your project management software), and let's get started on this journey together.

Tools and Technologies for Remote Collaboration

In today's digital age, there's no shortage of tools and technologies designed to make remote collaboration seamless and efficient. From video conferencing software to project management platforms, these tools are the glue that holds virtual teams together. But with so many options out there, it can be overwhelming to know where to start. That's why we've put together this comprehensive guide to the essential tools and technologies for remote collaboration.

1. Video Conferencing Software

- Zoom: This popular platform offers high-quality video and audio, screen sharing, and the ability to record meetings for later reference.
- Google Meet: Integrated with Google Workspace, Meet offers easy-to-join video calls, screen sharing, and real-time captions.
- Microsoft Teams: Part of the Microsoft 365 suite, Teams combines video conferencing, chat, and file sharing in one platform.
- Skype: One of the original video conferencing tools, Skype offers free video and voice calls, instant messaging, and screen sharing.

2. Project Management Platforms

- Asana: This user-friendly platform allows you to create tasks, assign them to team members, set deadlines, and track progress all in one place.
- Trello: With its visual, card-based interface, Trello is ideal for organizing tasks and workflows, especially for teams that prefer a more visual approach.

- Monday.com: This highly customizable platform offers a range of project management tools, including task tracking, timeline views, and automated workflows.
- Jira: Designed specifically for software development teams, Jira offers agile project management features like sprint planning, issue tracking, and reporting.

3. Communication Tools
- Slack: This popular messaging platform allows teams to communicate in real-time, share files, and integrate with a range of other tools and apps.
- Microsoft Teams: In addition to video conferencing, Teams offers robust chat and messaging features, including threaded conversations and the ability to create dedicated channels for specific topics or projects.
- Google Chat: Formerly known as Google Hangouts Chat, this messaging platform is integrated with Google Workspace and offers direct messaging, group chats, and the ability to create virtual rooms for specific topics or teams.

4. File Sharing and Collaboration
- Google Drive: Part of the Google Workspace suite, Drive offers secure cloud storage, real-time collaboration on documents, spreadsheets, and presentations, and the ability to easily share files with team members.
- Dropbox: This popular file sharing platform offers secure cloud storage, file syncing across devices, and the ability to collaborate on files in real-time.
- Microsoft OneDrive: Integrated with Microsoft 365, OneDrive offers secure cloud storage, file sharing, and real-time collaboration on Office documents.

5. Time Tracking and Productivity
- Toggl: This simple but powerful time tracking tool allows team members to track time spent on tasks, projects, and clients, and generates detailed reports for analysis and invoicing.
- RescueTime: This automated time tracking tool runs in the background and provides detailed insights into how team members are spending their time, helping to identify areas for improvement.
- Forest: This unique app gamifies productivity by allowing users to plant virtual trees when they focus on a task for a set amount of time, encouraging them to stay focused and avoid distractions.

6. Remote Access and Support
- TeamViewer: This powerful remote access tool allows team members to securely access and control each other's computers, making it easy to provide remote support and collaboration.
- LogMeIn: Similar to TeamViewer, LogMeIn offers remote access and support features, as well as the ability to host virtual meetings and share files securely.
- Splashtop: With its user-friendly interface and fast performance, Splashtop is a popular choice for remote access and support, particularly for IT teams supporting remote workers.

7. Password Management
- LastPass: This secure password manager allows teams to store and share passwords, ensuring that everyone has access to the tools and accounts they need without compromising security.

- Dashlane: Similar to LastPass, Dashlane offers secure password storage and sharing, as well as features like automatic password generation and a digital wallet for storing payment information.
- 1Password: With its user-friendly interface and robust security features, 1Password is a popular choice for teams looking to manage passwords and other sensitive information securely.

Choosing the right tools and technologies for your team will depend on your specific needs, preferences, and budget. But by investing in a suite of tools that covers the essential areas of collaboration - video conferencing, project management, communication, file sharing, time tracking, remote access, and password management - you'll be well-equipped to lead your virtual team to success.

Of course, tools and technologies are just one piece of the puzzle. To truly thrive as a remote project manager, you'll also need to cultivate the right mindset, communication skills, and leadership strategies. But with the right tools in your arsenal, you'll be off to a strong start.

So go ahead, take a deep dive into the world of remote collaboration tools. Experiment with different platforms, find what works best for your team, and don't be afraid to mix and match to create a custom toolkit that fits your unique needs. With the right tools and technologies at your fingertips, there's no limit to what your virtual team can achieve.

Establishing a Productive Remote Work Environment

When it comes to remote work, creating a productive environment is just as important as having the right tools and technologies. After all, you could have the most cutting-edge project management software, but if your team is working from cluttered, distracting home offices, their productivity will suffer. That's why establishing a productive remote work environment is a crucial piece of the puzzle for any successful virtual team.

So, what does a productive remote work environment look like? It's not just about having a dedicated office space (although that certainly helps). It's about creating a physical and mental space that promotes focus, creativity, and collaboration. Here are some key strategies for establishing a productive remote work environment:

1. **Encourage a dedicated workspace**
   - While not everyone has the luxury of a separate home office, encouraging your team to create a dedicated workspace can make a big difference in their productivity. This could be a corner of their living room, a spare bedroom, or even a clutter-free section of their kitchen table.
   - The key is to have a space that is solely dedicated to work, separate from the distractions of home life. This helps to create a mental boundary between work and personal time, making it easier to focus during work hours and unplug at the end of the day.

2. **Promote good ergonomics**
   - Just because your team is working from home doesn't mean they should be slouching on the couch with their laptop. Promoting good ergonomics is crucial for both productivity and long-term health.
   - Encourage your team to invest in a supportive chair, a desk or table at the proper height, and any necessary ergonomic accessories like a keyboard tray or monitor stand. You may even consider offering a stipend for home office equipment to ensure everyone has what they need to work comfortably and efficiently.

3. **Encourage natural light and fresh air**
   - Studies have shown that exposure to natural light and fresh air can boost mood, energy levels, and cognitive function. Encourage your team to set up their workspace near a window if possible, and to take breaks throughout the day to step outside and get some fresh air.
   - If natural light is limited, investing in a high-quality desk lamp or light therapy lamp can also help to regulate mood and energy levels.

4. **Minimize distractions**
   - Distractions are the enemy of productivity, and they can be especially prevalent in a home office setting. Encourage your team to identify and minimize distractions as much as possible.
   - This might mean setting clear boundaries with family members or roommates, using noise-cancelling headphones or a white noise machine to block out background noise, or using website and app blockers to limit social media and other online distractions during

work hours.

5. Encourage personalization
- While it's important to have a dedicated, clutter-free workspace, that doesn't mean it has to be sterile and impersonal. Encouraging your team to personalize their workspace with plants, artwork, or other meaningful items can help to create a sense of comfort and ownership, boosting motivation and productivity.
- Just be sure to strike a balance between personalization and clutter. A few thoughtfully chosen items can make a big difference, but too much clutter can be distracting and overwhelming.

6. Foster a sense of connection
- One of the biggest challenges of remote work is the sense of isolation and disconnection that can come from working alone. To combat this, it's important to foster a sense of connection and community within your virtual team.
- This might mean starting each day with a casual team check-in, creating virtual water cooler moments for socializing and team-building, or encouraging the use of video during meetings to create a sense of face-to-face connection.
- By fostering a sense of connection and belonging, you'll create a more supportive and collaborative work environment, even from a distance.

Establishing a productive remote work environment takes effort and intentionality, but it's well worth the investment. By encouraging dedicated workspaces, good ergonomics, natural light and fresh air, minimized distractions, personalization, and a sense of connection, you'll set your virtual team up for success.

Of course, what works for one team member may not work for another, so it's important to be flexible and adaptable. Encourage open communication and feedback, and be willing to make adjustments as needed to ensure everyone has the environment they need to thrive.

With a little creativity and a lot of intentionality, you can create a remote work environment that rivals even the most well-equipped office. And who knows - you may even find that your team is more productive and engaged than ever before, all from the comfort of their own homes.

Chapter 2
Key Skills for Remote Project Managers
Communication and Active Listening

As a remote project manager, communication is your superpower. It's the foundation upon which all other skills are built, and it's what keeps your virtual team connected, aligned, and moving forward. But when you're not sharing the same physical space, communication can also be one of your biggest challenges. That's why mastering the art of communication and active listening is absolutely essential for any remote project manager.

So, what does effective communication look like in a remote setting? It starts with being proactive and intentional. In a traditional office, you might be able to rely on casual hallway conversations or impromptu meetings to keep everyone on the same page. But in a remote setting, you need to be more deliberate about creating opportunities for communication.

This might mean:

1. **Establishing regular check-ins**
   - Set up daily or weekly stand-up meetings to give everyone a chance to share progress updates, ask questions, and align on priorities.
   - Use video conferencing to create a sense of face-to-face connection, even from a distance.

2. Using the right tools
- Choose communication tools that fit your team's needs and preferences, whether that's instant messaging, email, or project management software.
- Ensure everyone is trained on how to use the tools effectively, and establish clear guidelines for communication (e.g. using @mentions to get someone's attention, keeping conversations organized in dedicated channels).

3. Being clear and concise
- In a remote setting, it's easy for messages to get lost in translation or for important details to get buried in a long email chain. Strive for clarity and concision in all your communication.
- Use bullet points, numbered lists, and bolded key terms to make your messages easy to scan and digest.
- If a message is getting too long or complex, consider hopping on a quick video call instead.

4. Documenting everything
- In a remote setting, documentation is your friend. Make sure to record all important decisions, action items, and project updates in a central location that everyone can access.
- Use collaborative tools like Google Docs or Confluence to create living documents that can be updated in real-time.

But effective communication isn't just about how you convey information - it's also about how you receive it. That's where active listening comes in. Active listening is the practice of fully focusing on and engaging with the person speaking, rather than just passively hearing their words.

In a remote setting, active listening can be challenging because you don't have the benefit of reading body language or picking up on subtle nonverbal cues. That's why it's important to be extra intentional about showing that you're fully present and engaged in the conversation.

This might mean:

1. **Minimizing distractions**
   - Close out of other tabs and applications, put your phone on silent, and give the speaker your full attention.
   - If you're on a video call, make sure your camera is on and you're making eye contact (even if it's just with the camera).

2. **Using verbal and nonverbal cues**
   - Nod your head, smile, and use other nonverbal cues to show that you're engaged in the conversation.
   - Use verbal affirmations like "mm-hmm" or "I see" to show that you're actively listening.

3. **Reflecting and paraphrasing**
   - After the speaker has finished, reflect back what you heard to ensure you understood correctly.
   - Paraphrase key points in your own words to show that you're processing and internalizing the information.

4. **Asking clarifying questions**
   - If something is unclear or you need more information, don't be afraid to ask clarifying questions.
   - Use open-ended questions to encourage the speaker to elaborate and provide more context.

By combining proactive, intentional communication with active listening skills, you'll be well-equipped to lead your virtual team to success. You'll create a culture of open, transparent communication where everyone feels heard and valued, even from a distance.

Of course, communication and active listening are just one piece of the puzzle. As a remote project manager, you'll also need to master skills like time management, leadership, and adaptability (which we'll cover in more detail later). But by starting with a foundation of strong communication, you'll be setting yourself up for success in all other areas.

So take the time to hone your communication and active listening skills. Practice being proactive, clear, and concise in your messaging. Work on being fully present and engaged in every conversation. And most importantly, lead by example. By modeling effective communication and active listening yourself, you'll inspire your team to do the same.

With a little practice and a lot of intention, you'll be well on your way to mastering the art of communication and active listening in a remote setting. And trust us - your team (and your projects) will thank you for it.

Time Management and Organization

Time management and organization are critical skills for any project manager, but they become even more important in a remote setting. When you're not sharing the same physical space as your team, it's easy for tasks to fall through the cracks, deadlines to be missed, and priorities to become muddled. That's why having a system in place for managing your time and staying organized is absolutely essential.

So, what does effective time management and organization look like for a remote project manager? It starts with having a clear understanding of your priorities and goals. What are the most important tasks and projects on your plate? What deadlines are looming? What stakeholders need to be kept in the loop?

Once you have a clear picture of your priorities, it's time to put a plan in place. This might involve:

1. **Creating a project roadmap**
   - Break down large projects into smaller, more manageable tasks and milestones.
   - Create a visual roadmap that shows the timeline and dependencies for each task.
   - Share the roadmap with your team and stakeholders to ensure everyone is aligned on the big picture.

2. **Using a project management tool**
   - Choose a project management tool that fits your team's needs and workflow (e.g. Asana, Trello, Jira).

- Use the tool to create tasks, assign owners, set deadlines, and track progress.
- Integrate the tool with your other communication and collaboration platforms to keep everything in one place.

3. Time blocking your schedule
- Use a calendar or scheduling tool to block out dedicated time for specific tasks and projects.
- Be realistic about how much time each task will take, and build in buffer time for unexpected issues or interruptions.
- Communicate your schedule to your team so they know when you're available and when you're heads-down on focused work.

4. Prioritizing and delegating
- Use a prioritization framework like the Eisenhower Matrix to help you identify urgent vs. important tasks.
- Delegate tasks to team members based on their skills and availability, and provide clear instructions and expectations.
- Learn to say no to non-essential tasks or meetings that don't align with your priorities.

5. Taking breaks and avoiding burnout
- Build in regular breaks throughout your day to recharge and avoid burnout.
- Use techniques like the Pomodoro Method to work in focused sprints followed by short breaks.
- Encourage your team to do the same, and model good self-care habits yourself.

But time management and organization aren't just about your own individual workflow - they're also about how you communicate and collaborate with your team. In a remote setting, it's important to be extra clear and transparent about tasks, deadlines, and expectations.

This might involve:

1. **Setting clear agendas and outcomes for meetings**
   - Before each meeting, circulate a clear agenda that outlines the topics to be discussed and the desired outcomes.
   - Stick to the agenda during the meeting, and make sure to capture action items and next steps.
   - Follow up after the meeting with a summary and any relevant documents or resources.

2. **Providing regular progress updates**
   - Keep your team and stakeholders informed about project progress, challenges, and changes.
   - Use a regular cadence of updates (e.g. daily stand-ups, weekly status reports) to ensure everyone is on the same page.
   - Celebrate milestones and successes along the way to keep morale and motivation high.

3. **Establishing clear communication channels**
   - Make sure your team knows the best way to reach you for different types of questions or concerns (e.g. email for non-urgent issues, instant message for quick questions, phone or video call for complex discussions).

- Set expectations around response times and availability, and stick to them as much as possible.
- Encourage your team to do the same, and model good communication habits yourself.

By combining personal time management and organization strategies with clear communication and collaboration practices, you'll be well-equipped to keep your remote projects on track and your team aligned and productive.

Of course, time management and organization are ongoing practices, not one-time events. It's important to regularly review and adjust your strategies based on what's working and what's not. Don't be afraid to experiment with different tools and techniques until you find a system that works for you and your team.

And remember - perfection isn't the goal. There will always be unexpected issues and challenges that arise, and that's okay. The key is to stay flexible, adaptable, and focused on your priorities. With a solid foundation of time management and organization skills, you'll be better equipped to handle whatever comes your way.

So take the time to assess your current time management and organization practices. Identify areas for improvement, and start implementing some of the strategies we've discussed. And most importantly, be patient with yourself and your team. Developing new habits and routines takes time, but the payoff in terms of increased productivity, reduced stress, and better project outcomes is well worth the effort.

Leadership and Motivation

Leadership and motivation are the cornerstones of any successful project, but they can be particularly challenging in a remote setting. When you're not sharing the same physical space as your team, it's easy for communication breakdowns, misunderstandings, and disengagement to occur. That's why it's so important for remote project managers to be proactive and intentional about their leadership and motivation strategies.

So, what does effective leadership look like in a remote setting? At its core, it's about creating a vision, aligning your team around that vision, and empowering them to do their best work. This might involve:

1. Setting clear goals and expectations
- Communicate the big-picture objectives and key results for the project, and make sure everyone understands their role in achieving them.
- Break down larger goals into specific, measurable, achievable, relevant, and time-bound (SMART) objectives for each team member.
- Regularly review and adjust goals based on progress and changing circumstances.

2. Providing context and purpose
- Help your team understand how their work fits into the larger organizational strategy and mission.
- Communicate the "why" behind tasks and decisions, not just the "what" and "how."

- Celebrate milestones and successes along the way, and show appreciation for your team's hard work and contributions.

3. Empowering and trusting your team
- Give your team members the autonomy and resources they need to do their best work.
- Trust them to make decisions and solve problems on their own, while providing support and guidance when needed.
- Encourage experimentation and risk-taking, and create a safe space for learning and growth.

4. Being a coach and mentor
- Provide regular feedback and coaching to help your team members develop their skills and reach their full potential.
- Use a strengths-based approach, focusing on what each team member is naturally good at and helping them build on those strengths.
- Encourage peer-to-peer learning and collaboration, and create opportunities for team members to learn from each other.

But leadership is only one side of the coin - motivation is equally important. In a remote setting, it's easy for team members to feel isolated, disconnected, and disengaged from their work. That's why it's so important for remote project managers to be proactive about creating a motivating and engaging work environment.

This might involve:

1. **Creating a sense of belonging and connection**
   - Foster a sense of team identity and camaraderie through regular team-building activities and social interactions.
   - Use icebreakers, games, and other fun activities to help team members get to know each other on a personal level.
   - Encourage informal communication and "water cooler" conversations through dedicated chat channels or virtual coffee breaks.

2. **Recognizing and rewarding achievements**
   - Regularly acknowledge and celebrate individual and team successes, both big and small.
   - Use a variety of recognition and reward strategies, such as public shout-outs, bonus days off, or personalized gifts.
   - Encourage peer-to-peer recognition and appreciation through tools like Slack plugins or virtual kudos boards.

3. **Supporting work-life balance and well-being**
   - Encourage team members to set boundaries around their work hours and take regular breaks throughout the day.
   - Provide resources and support for mental health and well-being, such as access to meditation apps or virtual wellness workshops.
   - Model good self-care habits yourself, and prioritize your own work-life balance and well-being.

4. Providing opportunities for growth and development
- Offer training and development opportunities to help team members build new skills and advance their careers.
- Encourage team members to take on stretch assignments and leadership roles within the project.
- Create a culture of continuous learning and improvement, and encourage team members to share their knowledge and expertise with each other.

By combining effective leadership strategies with proactive motivation and engagement techniques, remote project managers can create a high-performing, highly motivated team that can tackle even the most complex and challenging projects.

Of course, every team is different, and what works for one group may not work for another. It's important to take the time to get to know your team members as individuals, understand their unique motivations and preferences, and tailor your leadership and motivation strategies accordingly.

And remember - leadership and motivation are not one-time events, but ongoing practices that require continuous attention and effort. It's important to regularly check in with your team members, solicit feedback and input, and adjust your approach as needed.

With a commitment to intentional leadership and proactive motivation, remote project managers can create a team culture that is engaged, productive, and resilient in the face of even the most challenging circumstances.

So take the time to assess your current leadership and motivation practices, identify areas for improvement, and start implementing some of the strategies we've discussed. Your team (and your projects) will thank you for it.

Adaptability and Problem-Solving

In the fast-paced, ever-changing world of remote project management, adaptability and problem-solving skills are absolutely essential. When you're leading a team from a distance, there are countless opportunities for things to go wrong - from technology glitches to communication breakdowns to unexpected changes in project scope or timelines. That's why it's so important for remote project managers to be able to think on their feet, adapt to changing circumstances, and find creative solutions to complex problems.

So, what does adaptability look like in practice? It starts with being flexible and open-minded. In a remote setting, things rarely go according to plan - and that's okay. The key is to be willing to pivot and adjust your approach as needed, rather than getting stuck in a rigid mindset or plan.

This might involve:

1. Embracing change and uncertainty
- Recognize that change is a constant in remote project management, and be willing to embrace it rather than resist it.
- Cultivate a mindset of curiosity and experimentation, and be open to trying new tools, techniques, and approaches.
- Communicate changes and uncertainties to your team in a transparent and proactive way, and involve them in the decision-making process wherever possible.

2. **Being proactive and anticipating challenges**
   - Continuously scan the horizon for potential risks and challenges, and develop contingency plans and mitigation strategies.
   - Use data and analytics to identify trends and patterns, and use that information to make informed decisions and course-correct as needed.
   - Foster a culture of continuous improvement and learning, and encourage your team to share their insights and ideas for improving processes and outcomes.

3. **Leveraging technology and tools**
   - Stay up-to-date on the latest project management and collaboration tools, and be willing to experiment with new technologies that could help your team work more efficiently and effectively.
   - Use automation and integration to streamline processes and reduce manual work, freeing up your team to focus on higher-value activities.
   - Provide training and support to help your team adopt and make the most of new tools and technologies.

But adaptability is only half the equation - problem-solving is equally important. In a remote setting, problems can arise at any time, and it's up to the project manager to find creative and effective solutions.

This might involve:

1. **Breaking down complex problems into smaller, more manageable parts**

- Use tools like mind mapping, fishbone diagrams, or the 5 Whys technique to visualize and analyze complex problems.
- Break down larger problems into smaller sub-problems, and assign them to team members with the relevant skills and expertise.
- Use a systematic, step-by-step approach to problem-solving, and document your process and findings along the way.

2. **Encouraging diverse perspectives and ideas**
   - Bring together team members with different backgrounds, skills, and perspectives to brainstorm and generate ideas.
   - Use techniques like lateral thinking, analogical reasoning, or the Six Thinking Hats to encourage creative and divergent thinking.
   - Create a psychologically safe environment where team members feel comfortable sharing their ideas and opinions, even if they're unconventional or contrarian.

3. **Experimenting and iterating**
   - Use a hypothesis-driven approach to problem-solving, and be willing to test and refine your ideas through rapid experimentation and iteration.
   - Use tools like A/B testing, prototyping, or pilot programs to quickly validate ideas and gather feedback.
   - Celebrate both successes and failures as opportunities for learning and improvement, and encourage your team to take calculated risks and learn from their mistakes.

4. Collaborating and communicating effectively

- Use collaborative problem-solving techniques like pair programming, design thinking, or agile methodologies to bring together diverse perspectives and skills.
- Foster open and transparent communication, and create channels for team members to share their ideas, concerns, and feedback.
- Use clear and concise language, active listening, and visual aids to ensure that everyone is on the same page and working towards the same goals.

By cultivating a mindset of adaptability and developing a toolkit of problem-solving techniques, remote project managers can navigate even the most complex and challenging situations with confidence and skill.

Of course, adaptability and problem-solving are not innate talents, but skills that can be developed and strengthened over time. It's important for remote project managers to invest in their own learning and development, whether through formal training programs, mentorship and coaching, or self-directed learning.

And remember - adaptability and problem-solving are not solo pursuits, but collaborative efforts that require the engagement and input of the entire team. By fostering a culture of adaptability, experimentation, and continuous improvement, remote project managers can create a team that is resilient, innovative, and able to tackle even the toughest challenges.

So take the time to assess your own adaptability and problem-solving skills, and identify areas for growth and development. Seek out new tools, techniques, and approaches, and be willing to experiment and take calculated risks. And most importantly, involve your team in the process, and create a culture of collaboration, communication, and continuous learning.

With a commitment to adaptability and a toolkit of problem-solving techniques, remote project managers can lead their teams to success, no matter what challenges come their way.

Part II
Managing Projects in a Remote Setting

Chapter 3
Project Planning and Initiation

Defining Project Scope and Objectives

Project planning and initiation are critical steps in any project, but they take on even greater importance in a remote setting. When you're not sharing the same physical space as your team, it's easy for misunderstandings and miscommunications to occur, leading to scope creep, missed deadlines, and other project pitfalls. That's why it's so important for remote project managers to be intentional and thorough in their project planning and initiation processes.

At the heart of project planning and initiation is defining the project scope and objectives. This is where you lay the foundation for the entire project, setting the stage for success and ensuring that everyone is aligned and working towards the same goals.

So, what does it mean to define project scope and objectives? Put simply, it's about clearly articulating what the project will (and will not) deliver, and what success looks like. This involves several key steps:

1. Identifying project stakeholders and their needs
- Conduct a stakeholder analysis to identify all the individuals and groups who have an interest in or influence over the project.
- Engage with stakeholders to understand their needs, expectations, and priorities.
- Document stakeholder requirements and expectations in a clear and concise way.

2. Defining project goals and objectives
- Work with stakeholders to define the high-level goals and objectives for the project.
- Use the SMART framework to ensure that objectives are Specific, Measurable, Achievable, Relevant, and Time-bound.
- Prioritize objectives based on their importance and urgency.

3. Determining project deliverables and requirements
- Break down project objectives into specific deliverables and requirements.
- Use techniques like user stories, use cases, or requirements documentation to clearly articulate what needs to be delivered.
- Validate deliverables and requirements with stakeholders to ensure alignment and buy-in.

4. Establishing project boundaries and constraints
- Clearly define what is in and out of scope for the project.
- Identify any constraints or limitations that may impact the project, such as budget, timeline, or resource availability.

- Communicate scope and constraints to all project team members and stakeholders.

5. Creating a project charter and plan
- Develop a project charter that summarizes the key elements of the project, including objectives, deliverables, scope, timeline, budget, and risks.
- Create a detailed project plan that breaks down the work into specific tasks, assignments, and milestones.
- Use tools like Gantt charts, roadmaps, or project management software to visualize and track progress.

By taking the time to thoroughly define project scope and objectives upfront, remote project managers can set their projects up for success and avoid many of the common pitfalls that can derail projects in a remote setting.

Of course, defining project scope and objectives is not a one-time event, but an ongoing process that requires regular review and refinement. As the project progresses, it's important to continually validate scope and objectives with stakeholders, and make adjustments as needed based on changing circumstances or new information.

It's also important to involve the entire project team in the scoping and planning process, to ensure that everyone has a shared understanding of the project goals and their roles and responsibilities in achieving them. This can be particularly challenging in a remote setting, where team members may be working across different time zones and communication channels.

To overcome these challenges, remote project managers can use a variety of techniques and tools, such as:
- Virtual whiteboarding and collaboration tools to facilitate real-time brainstorming and ideation.
- Video conferencing and screen sharing to walk through project plans and deliverables in detail.
- Asynchronous communication channels like email, chat, or project management software to keep everyone informed and aligned.
- Regular check-ins and status meetings to review progress, identify issues, and make course corrections as needed.

By combining thorough upfront planning with ongoing communication and collaboration, remote project managers can ensure that their projects stay on track and deliver the desired outcomes, even in the face of the unique challenges of remote work.

So if you're a remote project manager, take the time to invest in project planning and initiation, and particularly in defining project scope and objectives. It may seem like a lot of work upfront, but it will pay off in spades throughout the life of the project, and help you avoid many of the common pitfalls that can derail remote projects.

And remember - you don't have to do it alone. Involve your team, engage with stakeholders, and use the tools and techniques at your disposal to make the process as collaborative and effective as possible. With a solid foundation of well-defined scope and objectives, your remote projects will be set up for success from day one.

Creating a Project Charter and Plan

Once you've defined the project scope and objectives, it's time to create a project charter and plan. These are two essential documents that will guide the project from start to finish, and ensure that everyone is on the same page and working towards the same goals.

Let's start with the project charter. This is a high-level document that summarizes the key elements of the project, and serves as a "contract" between the project team and stakeholders. A typical project charter includes:

1. **Project overview and objectives**
   - A brief summary of the project, including its purpose, goals, and expected outcomes.
   - The specific objectives the project aims to achieve, using the SMART framework (Specific, Measurable, Achievable, Relevant, Time-bound).

2. **Project scope and deliverables**
   - A clear definition of what is in and out of scope for the project.
   - The specific deliverables the project will produce, along with their acceptance criteria.

3. **Project timeline and milestones**
   - The overall timeline for the project, including key milestones and deadlines.
   - Any dependencies or constraints that may impact the timeline.

4. Project budget and resources
- The total budget allocated for the project, broken down by category or phase.
- The resources (people, equipment, materials) required to complete the project.

5. Project risks and assumptions
- The key risks that could impact the project, along with mitigation strategies.
- Any assumptions or dependencies that the project relies on.

6. Project stakeholders and communication plan
- A list of all project stakeholders, along with their roles and responsibilities.
- A plan for how and when stakeholders will be engaged and communicated with throughout the project.

Creating a project charter is a collaborative process that involves input from all key stakeholders. It's important to take the time to review and refine the charter until everyone is aligned and in agreement.

Once the project charter is complete, it's time to create a detailed project plan. This is where you'll break down the high-level goals and deliverables from the charter into specific tasks, assignments, and timelines.

A typical project plan includes:

1. **Work Breakdown Structure (WBS)**
   - A hierarchical decomposition of the project scope into smaller, manageable tasks and sub-tasks.
   - Each task should be specific, measurable, and assignable to a team member or group.

2. **Task dependencies and sequences**
   - An analysis of how tasks are related to each other, and the order in which they need to be completed.
   - Identification of any critical path tasks that have no slack time and must be completed on schedule.

3. **Resource assignments and allocations**
   - The specific team members or groups responsible for completing each task.
   - An analysis of resource availability and capacity, to ensure that no one is overloaded or underutilized.

4. **Project schedule and timeline**
   - A detailed schedule showing the start and end dates for each task, along with any key milestones or deadlines.
   - A visual representation of the schedule, such as a Gantt chart or calendar view.

5. **Project budget and cost estimates**
   - A detailed breakdown of the project budget, showing the estimated cost for each task or phase.
   - A plan for tracking and managing costs throughout the project.

6. Risk management plan
- A detailed plan for identifying, assessing, and mitigating project risks.
- Contingency plans for dealing with issues or roadblocks that may arise.

7. Quality management plan
- A plan for ensuring that project deliverables meet the required quality standards.
- Processes for testing, reviewing, and approving deliverables before they are accepted.

Creating a detailed project plan is a time-consuming process, but it's essential for keeping the project on track and ensuring that nothing falls through the cracks. It's important to involve the entire project team in the planning process, to ensure that everyone understands their roles and responsibilities and has a chance to provide input and feedback.

Once the project plan is complete, it should be reviewed and approved by all key stakeholders, and then communicated to the entire project team. It's also important to establish a regular cadence of project status meetings and reports, to track progress against the plan and identify any issues or risks that need to be addressed.

In a remote setting, creating a project charter and plan can be particularly challenging, as team members may be working across different time zones and communication channels. To overcome these challenges, remote project managers can use a variety of tools and techniques, such as:

- Collaborative project management software like Asana, Trello, or Monday.com, which allow team members to create, assign, and track tasks in real-time.
- Virtual whiteboarding and mind mapping tools like Miro or Lucidchart, which facilitate real-time brainstorming and ideation.
- Video conferencing and screen sharing tools like Zoom or Skype, which allow team members to walk through project plans and deliverables in detail.
- Asynchronous communication channels like email, chat, or project management software, which keep everyone informed and aligned even when they're not working at the same time.

By combining a clear project charter with a detailed project plan, and using the right tools and techniques to facilitate collaboration and communication, remote project managers can set their projects up for success and ensure that everyone is working towards the same goals.

So if you're a remote project manager, don't skimp on the project charter and plan. Take the time to create these essential documents, involve your team in the process, and use them as your roadmap throughout the project. With a solid foundation in place, you'll be well-equipped to navigate the challenges of remote project management and deliver successful outcomes for your team and stakeholders.

Assembling Your Virtual Team

Now that you have a project charter and plan in place, it's time to assemble your virtual team. This is a critical step in any project, but it takes on even greater importance in a remote setting, where team members may be working across different time zones, cultures, and communication styles.

Assembling a high-performing virtual team requires careful planning, communication, and leadership. Here are some key steps to follow:

1. **Identify the skills and expertise needed**
   - Review the project charter and plan to identify the specific skills and expertise required to complete the project successfully.
   - Consider both technical skills (e.g. programming, design, writing) and soft skills (e.g. communication, collaboration, problem-solving).
   - Create a skills matrix or inventory to map out the skills and expertise of potential team members.

2. **Select team members based on fit and availability**
   - Use the skills matrix to identify potential team members who have the required skills and expertise.
   - Consider factors such as workload, availability, time zone, and cultural fit when selecting team members.
   - Aim for a diverse team with complementary skills and perspectives.

3. Clearly define roles and responsibilities
- Create a RACI (Responsible, Accountable, Consulted, Informed) matrix or similar tool to clearly define the roles and responsibilities of each team member.
- Ensure that every task and deliverable has a clear owner and that everyone understands what is expected of them.
- Communicate roles and responsibilities to the entire team and stakeholders.

4. Establish communication and collaboration protocols
- Determine the primary communication channels and tools the team will use (e.g. email, chat, video conferencing).
- Set expectations for response times, availability, and communication style.
- Establish protocols for collaboration, such as using version control for documents and code, or using project management software to track tasks and deadlines.

5. Foster team bonding and trust
- Take the time to introduce team members to each other and allow for casual conversation and relationship-building.
- Use icebreakers, team-building activities, or virtual social events to help team members get to know each other on a personal level.
- Encourage open communication, active listening, and constructive feedback among team members.

6. Provide training and support
- Ensure that all team members have the necessary tools, resources, and access to complete their work.

- Provide training or guidance on any new tools, processes, or protocols the team will be using.
- Offer ongoing support and coaching to help team members develop their skills and overcome challenges.

Assembling a virtual team is not a one-time event, but an ongoing process that requires regular attention and maintenance. It's important to continuously assess team dynamics, communication, and performance, and make adjustments as needed to ensure that the team is working effectively and efficiently.

In a remote setting, assembling a virtual team can be particularly challenging, as team members may have different working styles, communication preferences, and cultural backgrounds. To overcome these challenges, remote project managers can use a variety of strategies, such as:

- Using personality assessments or team-building tools like the Myers-Briggs Type Indicator or the Clifton StrengthsFinder to help team members understand and appreciate each other's strengths and working styles.
- Establishing a team charter or working agreement that outlines the team's values, norms, and expectations for communication and collaboration.
- Providing cross-cultural training or resources to help team members navigate cultural differences and build trust and understanding.
- Using video conferencing and other rich communication channels to facilitate face-to-face interaction and build personal connections among team members.

- Celebrating team successes and milestones, and recognizing individual contributions and achievements.

By taking a thoughtful and proactive approach to assembling and managing a virtual team, remote project managers can create a high-performing and cohesive team that is able to work together effectively and deliver outstanding results.

So if you're a remote project manager, don't underestimate the importance of assembling the right team. Take the time to identify the skills and expertise you need, select team members based on fit and availability, clearly define roles and responsibilities, establish communication and collaboration protocols, foster team bonding and trust, and provide ongoing training and support. With a strong and well-supported virtual team in place, you'll be well-equipped to tackle even the most complex and challenging projects with confidence and success.

Conducting Effective Kick-Off Meetings

Once you've assembled your virtual team, it's time to officially kick off the project with a kick-off meeting. This is a critical event that sets the tone for the entire project and ensures that everyone is aligned and excited about the work ahead.

In a remote setting, conducting an effective kick-off meeting can be particularly challenging, as team members may be joining from different locations, time zones, and technology setups. However, with careful planning and facilitation, you can create a kick-off meeting that engages and energizes your team, and sets the project up for success.

Here are some key steps to follow when conducting a remote kick-off meeting:

1. **Set clear objectives and agenda**
   - Determine the specific goals and objectives of the kick-off meeting, such as reviewing the project charter and plan, clarifying roles and responsibilities, or building team rapport.
   - Create a detailed agenda that allocates time for each topic or activity, and share it with the team in advance.
   - Assign specific team members to lead or facilitate each agenda item, to ensure that the meeting stays on track and everyone has a chance to participate.

2. **Choose the right technology and tools**
   - Select a video conferencing platform that is reliable, user-friendly, and accessible to all team members.

- Test the technology in advance to ensure that audio, video, and screen sharing are working properly.
- Use collaborative tools like virtual whiteboards, mind maps, or polls to facilitate interaction and engagement during the meeting.

3. Establish meeting norms and expectations
- Set clear expectations for participation, such as keeping cameras on, muting microphones when not speaking, and using the chat or "raise hand" feature to ask questions or make comments.
- Encourage active listening, respectful communication, and constructive feedback among team members.
- Establish a "parking lot" or action item tracker to capture ideas or issues that come up during the meeting but require follow-up or further discussion.

4. Start with introductions and icebreakers
- Take the time to introduce each team member and their role on the project, even if they have worked together before.
- Use icebreakers or team-building activities to help team members get to know each other on a personal level and build rapport.
- Encourage team members to share their communication preferences, working styles, and any other relevant information that will help the team work together effectively.

5. **Review project charter and plan**
   - Walk through the key elements of the project charter, including the project objectives, scope, deliverables, timeline, and budget.
   - Review the project plan, including the work breakdown structure, task assignments, and milestones.
   - Clarify any questions or concerns team members may have about the project scope, timeline, or resources.

6. **Discuss roles and responsibilities**
   - Review the RACI matrix or similar tool that outlines the roles and responsibilities of each team member.
   - Ensure that every team member understands what is expected of them and how their work fits into the larger project goals.
   - Encourage team members to ask questions or raise concerns about their roles or workload.

7. **Establish communication and collaboration protocols**
   - Discuss the primary communication channels and tools the team will use, such as email, chat, or project management software.
   - Set expectations for response times, availability, and communication style.
   - Establish protocols for collaboration, such as using version control for documents and code, or using project management software to track tasks and deadlines.

8. **Close with next steps and action items**
   - Summarize the key takeaways and decisions from the meeting.

- Assign clear next steps and action items to specific team members, with deadlines and deliverables.
- Schedule regular check-ins and status meetings to keep the team informed and aligned throughout the project.

Conducting an effective kick-off meeting is just the beginning of a successful project. It's important to follow up after the meeting with a summary of key points and action items, and to continue to foster open communication and collaboration among team members throughout the project.

In a remote setting, it's also important to be aware of the unique challenges and opportunities that come with virtual meetings. For example, remote meetings can be more efficient and focused than in-person meetings, as there are fewer distractions and side conversations. However, they can also feel less personal and engaging, as team members may be tempted to multitask or tune out.

To overcome these challenges, remote project managers can use a variety of strategies, such as:
- Using breakout rooms or small group discussions to facilitate more intimate and focused conversations.
- Encouraging team members to use video and non-verbal cues like nodding or thumbs up to show engagement and agreement.
- Building in breaks or energizers to help team members stay focused and motivated throughout the meeting.
- Following up with individual team members after the meeting to check in on their understanding and buy-in.

By conducting an effective kick-off meeting and continuing to foster open communication and collaboration throughout the project, remote project managers can set their teams up for success and ensure that everyone is aligned and motivated to achieve the project goals.

So if you're a remote project manager, don't underestimate the power of a well-planned and well-executed kick-off meeting. Take the time to set clear objectives and agenda, choose the right technology and tools, establish meeting norms and expectations, start with introductions and icebreakers, review the project charter and plan, discuss roles and responsibilities, establish communication and collaboration protocols, and close with next steps and action items. With a strong foundation in place, you'll be well-equipped to lead your virtual team to success and deliver outstanding results.

Chapter 4
Project Execution and Monitoring
Assigning Tasks and Responsibilities

Once you've kicked off the project and established a strong foundation, it's time to dive into the execution and monitoring phase. This is where the rubber meets the road, and where your team's hard work and collaboration will determine the success or failure of the project.

One of the most critical aspects of project execution and monitoring is assigning tasks and responsibilities. This is where you take the high-level goals and deliverables from the project charter and plan and break them down into specific, actionable tasks that team members can execute on a day-to-day basis.

Assigning tasks and responsibilities effectively is both an art and a science. Here are some key steps to follow:

1. Break down deliverables into tasks
- Review the project plan and work breakdown structure to identify the specific deliverables and milestones that need to be achieved.
- Break down each deliverable into smaller, more manageable tasks that can be completed by individual team members or small groups.
- Ensure that each task is specific, measurable, and time-bound, with clear acceptance criteria and dependencies.

2. Assign tasks based on skills and availability
- Review the skills matrix or inventory to identify which team members have the necessary skills and expertise to complete each task.
- Consider factors such as workload, availability, and development goals when assigning tasks to team members.
- Ensure that every team member has a balanced workload and that no one is overloaded or underutilized.

3. Communicate assignments clearly and consistently
- Use a project management tool or platform to create and assign tasks to team members, with clear due dates, priorities, and dependencies.
- Communicate assignments to team members in multiple ways, such as through email, chat, or video conferencing, to ensure that everyone is aware of their responsibilities.
- Provide team members with any necessary resources, information, or context they need to complete their tasks successfully.

4. Monitor progress and provide feedback
- Use project management software or regular check-ins to monitor progress on tasks and deliverables.
- Provide regular feedback and coaching to team members to help them stay on track and overcome any obstacles or challenges.
- Celebrate successes and milestones along the way to keep the team motivated and engaged.

5. Adjust assignments as needed
- Be prepared to adjust task assignments and priorities as the project evolves and new information or challenges arise.
- Communicate any changes or updates to the team clearly and consistently, and ensure that everyone understands the rationale behind the changes.
- Continuously assess team workload and capacity, and make adjustments as needed to ensure that everyone is working efficiently and effectively.

Assigning tasks and responsibilities effectively is critical for keeping the project on track and ensuring that everyone is working towards the same goals. However, it's important to remember that assignments are not set in stone, and that flexibility and adaptability are key to successful project execution and monitoring.

In a remote setting, assigning tasks and responsibilities can be particularly challenging, as team members may be working across different time zones and communication channels. To overcome these challenges, remote project managers can use a variety of strategies, such as:

- Using collaborative project management software like Asana, Trello, or Monday.com to create, assign, and track tasks in real-time.
- Establishing clear communication protocols and channels for discussing tasks and deliverables, such as daily stand-up meetings or dedicated Slack channels.

- Providing team members with the necessary tools and resources to complete their tasks remotely, such as access to cloud-based file storage or virtual meeting software.
- Encouraging team members to proactively communicate their progress, challenges, and needs, and to ask for help or clarification when needed.

By assigning tasks and responsibilities effectively and continuously monitoring and adjusting assignments as needed, remote project managers can ensure that their teams are working efficiently and effectively towards the project goals.

So if you're a remote project manager, don't underestimate the importance of effective task assignment and monitoring. Take the time to break down deliverables into specific, actionable tasks, assign tasks based on skills and availability, communicate assignments clearly and consistently, monitor progress and provide feedback, and adjust assignments as needed. With a proactive and flexible approach to task management, you'll be well-equipped to keep your virtual team on track and deliver outstanding results.

Tracking Progress and Milestones

Once you've assigned tasks and responsibilities to your team members, it's crucial to track progress and milestones throughout the project. This allows you to stay on top of how the project is advancing, identify any potential issues or roadblocks, and make informed decisions to keep the project on track.

Tracking progress and milestones effectively requires a combination of tools, processes, and communication. Here are some key steps to follow:

1. **Establish clear metrics and KPIs**
   - Define clear, measurable metrics and key performance indicators (KPIs) that align with the project goals and objectives.
   - Examples might include completed tasks, delivered features, user adoption rates, or customer satisfaction scores.
   - Ensure that the entire team understands the metrics and KPIs and how they will be measured and reported.

2. **Use project management tools**
   - Utilize project management software or tools to track progress on tasks, deliverables, and milestones.
   - Tools like Asana, Trello, or Jira allow you to create and assign tasks, set due dates and dependencies, and track completion status in real-time.
   - Ensure that all team members are trained on how to use the tools effectively and consistently.

3. **Conduct regular status meetings**
   - Schedule regular status meetings or check-ins with the team to review progress, identify issues, and make decisions.
   - Use a consistent meeting format or agenda, such as a daily stand-up or weekly status report, to ensure that all relevant information is covered.
   - Encourage team members to come prepared with updates, questions, and concerns, and to actively participate in the discussion.

4. **Visualize progress with dashboards and reports**
   - Create visual dashboards or reports that display key metrics, milestones, and progress over time.
   - Use charts, graphs, or color-coding to make the information easy to understand and interpret at a glance.
   - Share the dashboards or reports with stakeholders and team members to keep everyone informed and aligned.

5. **Celebrate milestones and successes**
   - Recognize and celebrate key milestones and successes along the way, such as completing a major deliverable or reaching a significant metric.
   - Use virtual meetings, email announcements, or social media posts to acknowledge and appreciate the team's hard work and achievements.
   - Encourage team members to share their own successes and learnings with each other, and to provide peer recognition and support.

6. Identify and address issues proactively
- Regularly review progress data and metrics to identify any potential issues or roadblocks that may impact the project.
- Proactively communicate any issues or concerns to the team and stakeholders, along with proposed solutions or mitigation strategies.
- Work collaboratively with the team to develop and implement corrective actions, and to adjust plans or assignments as needed to keep the project on track.

Tracking progress and milestones effectively is essential for keeping the project on schedule, within budget, and aligned with the overall goals and objectives. However, it's important to remember that tracking is not an end in itself, but rather a means to facilitate communication, decision-making, and continuous improvement.

In a remote setting, tracking progress and milestones can be particularly challenging, as team members may be working across different time zones and communication channels. To overcome these challenges, remote project managers can use a variety of strategies, such as:

- Establishing clear communication protocols and expectations for reporting progress and issues, such as daily check-ins or weekly status reports.
- Using collaborative project management tools that allow team members to update tasks and deliverables in real-time, regardless of location or time zone.

- Leveraging video conferencing and screen sharing to conduct virtual status meetings and demos, and to facilitate face-to-face communication and collaboration.
- Creating a culture of transparency and accountability, where team members feel comfortable sharing both successes and challenges, and where everyone is committed to working together to achieve the project goals.

By tracking progress and milestones effectively and using the data to inform decision-making and continuous improvement, remote project managers can keep their virtual teams on track and deliver high-quality results.

So if you're a remote project manager, make tracking progress and milestones a priority. Establish clear metrics and KPIs, use project management tools, conduct regular status meetings, visualize progress with dashboards and reports, celebrate milestones and successes, and identify and address issues proactively. By staying on top of project progress and using the data to drive action and improvement, you'll be well-equipped to lead your virtual team to success.

Managing Project Budgets and Resources

In addition to tracking progress and milestones, managing project budgets and resources is another critical responsibility of a project manager. This involves ensuring that the project has the necessary financial, human, and material resources to achieve its goals, while also staying within the allocated budget and timeline.

Managing project budgets and resources effectively requires a combination of planning, monitoring, and communication. Here are some key steps to follow:

1. **Develop a detailed budget plan**
   - Create a comprehensive budget plan that outlines all the anticipated expenses and costs associated with the project.
   - Break down the budget into specific categories, such as personnel, equipment, materials, travel, and contingency funds.
   - Ensure that the budget aligns with the project scope, timeline, and deliverables, and that it has been reviewed and approved by relevant stakeholders.

2. **Allocate resources based on priorities and needs**
   - Review the project plan and work breakdown structure to identify the specific resources needed for each task and deliverable.
   - Allocate resources based on the priority and criticality of each task, as well as the skills and availability of team members.

- Ensure that resources are being utilized efficiently and effectively, and that there is no duplication or waste of effort.

3. Monitor and control expenses
- Regularly review and monitor actual expenses against the budget plan, using financial tracking tools or software.
- Identify any variances or discrepancies between planned and actual expenses, and investigate the root causes.
- Take corrective actions as needed to bring expenses back in line with the budget, such as reducing scope, reallocating resources, or securing additional funding.

4. Manage resource capacity and utilization
- Track the availability and utilization of team members and other resources using resource management tools or spreadsheets.
- Identify any over- or under-allocation of resources, and make adjustments as needed to ensure that everyone is working efficiently and effectively.
- Communicate any changes or updates to resource assignments or schedules to the team and stakeholders, and ensure that everyone understands the rationale and impact.

5. Forecast and re-forecast regularly
- Regularly review and update the budget and resource forecasts based on actual data and progress to date.
- Use earned value management (EVM) or other forecasting techniques to predict future expenses and resource needs based on current performance.

- Communicate any significant variances or changes to the budget or resource plan to the team and stakeholders, along with proposed solutions or mitigation strategies.

6. **Collaborate and communicate with stakeholders**
- Work closely with project stakeholders, such as sponsors, clients, and finance teams, to ensure that the budget and resource plan aligns with their expectations and constraints.
- Provide regular updates and reports on budget and resource utilization to stakeholders, using clear and concise language and visuals.
- Proactively communicate any issues or risks related to budget or resources, and work collaboratively with stakeholders to develop solutions and make informed decisions.

Managing project budgets and resources effectively is critical for ensuring that the project stays on track and delivers the intended value and benefits. However, it's important to remember that budgets and resources are not fixed, and that flexibility and adaptability are key to successful project management.

In a remote setting, managing project budgets and resources can be particularly challenging, as team members may be working across different locations, systems, and processes. To overcome these challenges, remote project managers can use a variety of strategies, such as:

- Using cloud-based financial and resource management tools that allow team members to access and update data in real-time, regardless of location.
- Establishing clear policies and procedures for expense tracking, reimbursement, and approval, and communicating these to all team members.
- Leveraging video conferencing and screen sharing to conduct budget and resource planning meetings, and to facilitate face-to-face communication and collaboration.
- Creating a culture of transparency and accountability, where team members understand the importance of staying within budget and utilizing resources efficiently, and where everyone is committed to finding creative solutions to budget and resource challenges.

By managing project budgets and resources effectively and collaborating closely with stakeholders and team members, remote project managers can ensure that their virtual teams have the necessary resources to deliver high-quality results, while also staying within the constraints of the project.

So if you're a remote project manager, don't overlook the importance of budget and resource management. Develop a detailed budget plan, allocate resources based on priorities and needs, monitor and control expenses, manage resource capacity and utilization, forecast and re-forecast regularly, and collaborate and communicate with stakeholders. By staying on top of the financial and human aspects of the project and making informed decisions based on data and input, you'll be well-equipped to lead your virtual team to success while also delivering value to the organization.

Handling Project Changes and Risks

No matter how well you plan and execute a project, changes and risks are inevitable. As a project manager, it's your responsibility to anticipate, identify, and respond to these changes and risks in a way that minimizes their impact on the project and ensures that the project stays on track and delivers the intended value.

Handling project changes and risks effectively requires a combination of proactive planning, ongoing monitoring, and effective communication. Here are some key steps to follow:

1. **Develop a change management plan**
   - Create a formal change management plan that outlines the process for identifying, evaluating, and implementing changes to the project.
   - Define clear roles and responsibilities for change management, including who has the authority to request, approve, and implement changes.
   - Establish criteria for determining whether a change is necessary, feasible, and beneficial, and how it will be prioritized and communicated to stakeholders.

2. **Identify and assess risks**
   - Conduct a thorough risk assessment to identify potential risks and uncertainties that could impact the project, such as technical, financial, legal, or environmental risks.
   - Evaluate each risk based on its likelihood and potential impact, and prioritize risks based on their overall severity and urgency.

- Develop a risk register or matrix to document and track identified risks, along with their status, owner, and mitigation strategies.

3. **Develop risk mitigation and contingency plans**
   - For each identified risk, develop a mitigation plan that outlines the steps to be taken to prevent or reduce the likelihood and impact of the risk.
   - Identify specific triggers or thresholds that will prompt the implementation of the mitigation plan, and assign clear roles and responsibilities for executing the plan.
   - Develop contingency plans for high-impact risks that cannot be fully mitigated, outlining the steps to be taken to minimize the damage and recover from the risk if it occurs.

4. **Monitor and control changes and risks**
   - Regularly review and update the change management plan and risk register based on actual data and progress to date.
   - Monitor the project for any new or evolving risks or changes, and assess their potential impact on the project scope, timeline, budget, and quality.
   - Implement approved changes and risk mitigation plans as needed, and communicate the impact and rationale to the team and stakeholders.

5. **Communicate and collaborate with stakeholders**
   - Engage project stakeholders, such as sponsors, clients, and team members, in the change and risk management process, and seek their input and feedback.

- Provide regular updates and reports on changes and risks to stakeholders, using clear and concise language and visuals.
- Work collaboratively with stakeholders to develop and implement solutions to changes and risks, and to ensure that the project remains aligned with their expectations and needs.

6. Learn and adapt from changes and risks
- Use changes and risks as opportunities to learn and improve the project management process and outcomes.
- Conduct post-mortem reviews or retrospectives after significant changes or risks occur, to identify lessons learned and best practices.
- Incorporate these lessons and practices into future project planning and execution, and share them with the wider project management community.

Handling project changes and risks effectively is critical for ensuring that the project stays on track and delivers the intended value and benefits, even in the face of unexpected challenges and opportunities. However, it's important to remember that change and risk management is not a one-time event, but an ongoing process that requires continuous attention and adaptation.

In a remote setting, handling project changes and risks can be particularly challenging, as team members may be working across different locations, time zones, and cultures, and may have limited face-to-face interaction and communication. To overcome these challenges, remote project managers can use a variety of strategies, such as:

- Using cloud-based project management and collaboration tools that allow team members to access and update change and risk data in real-time, regardless of location.
- Establishing clear communication protocols and channels for discussing and escalating changes and risks, such as daily stand-ups, risk review meetings, or dedicated Slack channels.
- Leveraging video conferencing and screen sharing to conduct virtual change and risk management meetings, and to facilitate face-to-face communication and collaboration.
- Creating a culture of transparency, trust, and accountability, where team members feel comfortable raising and discussing changes and risks, and where everyone is committed to working together to find solutions and make informed decisions.

By handling project changes and risks effectively and collaboratively, remote project managers can help their virtual teams navigate the challenges and opportunities of the project landscape, and deliver high-quality results that meet or exceed stakeholder expectations.

So if you're a remote project manager, make change and risk management a priority. Develop a change management plan, identify and assess risks, develop risk mitigation and contingency plans, monitor and control changes and risks, communicate and collaborate with stakeholders, and learn and adapt from changes and risks. By staying proactive, flexible, and focused on delivering value, you'll be well-equipped to lead your virtual team through the ups and downs of the project journey, and emerge stronger and more successful on the other side.

Chapter 5
Project Communication and Collaboration
Establishing Communication Protocols

Effective communication and collaboration are the lifeblood of any successful project, but they become even more critical in a remote setting where team members may be working across different locations, time zones, and cultures. As a remote project manager, it's your responsibility to establish clear and consistent communication protocols that enable your team to work together efficiently, share information and ideas, and deliver high-quality results.

Establishing communication protocols involves defining the channels, frequency, and norms for communication within the project team and with external stakeholders. Here are some key steps to follow:

1. **Identify communication needs and preferences**
   - Conduct a communication needs assessment to identify the types of information that need to be communicated, the frequency and timing of communication, and the preferred channels and formats for communication.
   - Consider the different communication styles and preferences of team members, such as verbal vs. written, synchronous vs. asynchronous, or formal vs. informal.
   - Identify any specific communication requirements or constraints, such as language barriers, technical limitations, or confidentiality concerns.

2. Define communication channels and tools
- Based on the communication needs assessment, define the primary channels and tools for communication within the project team, such as email, instant messaging, video conferencing, project management software, or shared documents.
- Ensure that all team members have access to and are trained on the selected communication tools, and that they understand how and when to use each tool.
- Establish backup or alternate communication channels in case of technical issues or emergencies, and ensure that all team members know how to access and use them.

3. Establish communication norms and guidelines
- Develop clear and concise guidelines for communication within the project team, covering aspects such as response times, meeting etiquette, document naming and version control, and escalation procedures.
- Ensure that all team members understand and agree to follow the communication guidelines, and that they are held accountable for doing so.
- Model and reinforce the desired communication behaviors and norms, and provide feedback and coaching to team members who may need support or guidance.

4. Schedule regular communication touchpoints
- Establish a regular cadence of communication touchpoints, such as daily stand-ups, weekly status meetings, or monthly progress reviews, to ensure that all team members are informed and aligned on project progress, issues, and priorities.

- Use a consistent agenda and format for each touchpoint, and ensure that all team members come prepared to share updates, ask questions, and provide feedback.
- Document and share meeting notes and action items, and follow up on any outstanding items or decisions in a timely manner.

5. Foster open and inclusive communication
- Encourage open and honest communication within the project team, and create a safe and inclusive environment where all team members feel comfortable sharing their ideas, concerns, and feedback.
- Actively listen to and acknowledge the perspectives and contributions of all team members, and ensure that everyone has an equal opportunity to participate and be heard.
- Address any communication breakdowns or conflicts in a timely and constructive manner, and work with the team to identify root causes and develop solutions.

6. Adapt and improve communication over time
- Regularly solicit feedback from team members and stakeholders on the effectiveness and efficiency of project communication, and use this feedback to identify areas for improvement.
- Be open to adapting and evolving the communication protocols and tools over time, based on changing project needs, team dynamics, or external factors.
- Celebrate and share communication successes and best practices, and encourage team members to learn from and build on each other's strengths and experiences.

Establishing effective communication protocols is critical for ensuring that the project team can work together seamlessly and deliver high-quality results, even in a remote setting. However, it's important to remember that communication is not a one-size-fits-all approach, and that different team members and stakeholders may have different communication needs and preferences.

To overcome these challenges, remote project managers can use a variety of strategies, such as:

- Conducting regular communication check-ins and surveys to assess team members' satisfaction and engagement with project communication, and to identify areas for improvement.
- Using a variety of communication channels and formats, such as written, verbal, visual, and interactive, to cater to different learning and communication styles.
- Providing communication training and support to team members who may need help with specific tools, techniques, or cultural norms.
- Encouraging team members to take ownership of and initiative in project communication, and to propose and implement their own ideas for improving collaboration and information sharing.

By establishing clear, consistent, and inclusive communication protocols, and by adapting and improving them over time, remote project managers can help their virtual teams work together effectively and efficiently, and deliver results that meet or exceed stakeholder expectations.

So if you're a remote project manager, make communication and collaboration a top priority. Identify communication needs and preferences, define communication channels and tools, establish communication norms and guidelines, schedule regular communication touchpoints, foster open and inclusive communication, and adapt and improve communication over time. By creating a culture of transparency, trust, and teamwork, you'll be well-equipped to lead your virtual team to success, no matter where in the world they may be.

Running Productive Virtual Meetings

In a remote project setting, virtual meetings are a critical tool for bringing team members together, sharing information and ideas, and making decisions. However, virtual meetings can also be a source of frustration and inefficiency if they are not planned and facilitated effectively. As a remote project manager, it's your responsibility to ensure that virtual meetings are productive, engaging, and valuable for all participants.

Running productive virtual meetings involves a combination of careful planning, active facilitation, and follow-up. Here are some key steps to follow:

1. Define the purpose and agenda
- Clearly define the purpose and objectives of the meeting, and communicate them to all participants in advance.
- Develop a concise and focused agenda that outlines the topics to be discussed, the expected outcomes, and the time allocated for each item.
- Prioritize agenda items based on their importance and urgency, and ensure that there is enough time to cover all essential topics without rushing or running over.

2. Select the right tools and technology
- Choose a reliable and user-friendly virtual meeting platform that supports the necessary features and functions, such as video conferencing, screen sharing, and chat.
- Test the technology in advance to ensure that it works smoothly and that all participants have the necessary access and instructions.

- Provide technical support and guidance to participants who may need help with the meeting platform or tools.

3. **Prepare and distribute materials**
   - Prepare any necessary materials, such as presentations, documents, or data, and distribute them to participants in advance of the meeting.
   - Ensure that all materials are clear, concise, and relevant to the meeting purpose and agenda, and that they are accessible and easy to navigate.
   - Encourage participants to review the materials before the meeting and come prepared with questions, comments, or feedback.

4. **Set expectations and norms**
   - Establish clear expectations and norms for participation and behavior during the meeting, such as muting microphones when not speaking, raising hands to ask questions, or using chat for side conversations.
   - Communicate the meeting rules and guidelines to all participants in advance, and ensure that they are understood and agreed upon.
   - Model the desired behaviors and norms during the meeting, and gently remind participants who may need a reminder.

5. **Facilitate active participation and engagement**
   - Start the meeting with a brief check-in or icebreaker to build rapport and create a positive atmosphere.

- Use a variety of facilitation techniques, such as polling, breakout rooms, or interactive exercises, to encourage active participation and engagement from all participants.
- Encourage participants to ask questions, share ideas, and provide feedback, and ensure that everyone has an equal opportunity to contribute.

6. Manage time and focus
- Keep the meeting on track and on time by following the agenda and enforcing time limits for each item.
- Use timeboxing or other techniques to ensure that discussions stay focused and productive, and that tangents or side conversations are minimized.
- Be prepared to adjust the agenda or timing as needed based on the flow and needs of the meeting, while still ensuring that all essential topics are covered.

7. Summarize and follow up
- End the meeting with a clear summary of the key points, decisions, and action items, and ensure that all participants are aligned and committed.
- Distribute meeting notes and action items to all participants in a timely manner, and ensure that they are clear, complete, and actionable.
- Follow up with participants as needed to ensure that action items are completed, and that any outstanding questions or issues are addressed.

Running productive virtual meetings is critical for ensuring that the project team can communicate and collaborate effectively, even when working remotely. However, it's important to remember that virtual meetings can be challenging and draining, especially if they are long, complex, or poorly planned.

To overcome these challenges, remote project managers can use a variety of strategies, such as:

- Keeping meetings as short and focused as possible, and only inviting participants who are essential to the meeting purpose and agenda.
- Using asynchronous communication channels, such as email or project management software, for information sharing and status updates, and reserving meetings for discussion, decision-making, and problem-solving.
- Providing regular breaks and opportunities for informal socializing and team-building, to help participants stay energized and engaged.
- Seeking feedback and input from participants on how to improve the effectiveness and efficiency of virtual meetings, and using this feedback to continuously refine and adapt the meeting process.

By running productive virtual meetings that are well-planned, actively facilitated, and followed up on, remote project managers can help their virtual teams stay connected, aligned, and motivated, and deliver high-quality results that meet or exceed stakeholder expectations.

So if you're a remote project manager, make virtual meetings a priority. Define the purpose and agenda, select the right tools and technology, prepare and distribute materials, set expectations and norms, facilitate active participation and engagement, manage time and focus, and summarize and follow up. By creating a culture of effective and efficient virtual collaboration, you'll be well-equipped to lead your virtual team to success, no matter how dispersed or diverse they may be.

Using Collaboration Tools Effectively

In a remote project setting, collaboration tools are essential for enabling team members to work together seamlessly, share information and ideas, and deliver high-quality results. However, collaboration tools can also be a source of confusion, duplication, and inefficiency if they are not used effectively. As a remote project manager, it's your responsibility to ensure that collaboration tools are selected, implemented, and used in a way that supports the project goals and enhances team productivity.

Using collaboration tools effectively involves a combination of careful selection, clear communication, and ongoing support. Here are some key steps to follow:

1. **Identify collaboration needs and requirements**
   - Conduct a collaboration needs assessment to identify the types of activities and deliverables that require collaboration, the frequency and intensity of collaboration, and the preferences and constraints of team members.
   - Consider the different collaboration modes and channels that may be needed, such as document sharing, task management, video conferencing, or instant messaging.
   - Identify any specific collaboration requirements or constraints, such as security, accessibility, or integration with existing tools and systems.

2. Select the right collaboration tools
- Based on the collaboration needs assessment, select a suite of collaboration tools that meet the project requirements and align with the team's preferences and skills.
- Consider factors such as ease of use, reliability, scalability, cost, and compatibility with existing tools and systems when selecting collaboration tools.
- Involve team members in the tool selection process, and ensure that they have an opportunity to provide input and feedback on the tools being considered.

3. Establish clear guidelines and protocols
- Develop clear and concise guidelines for how each collaboration tool should be used, including the purpose, scope, and expectations for each tool.
- Establish protocols for how information should be shared, stored, and accessed within each tool, and ensure that all team members understand and agree to these protocols.
- Define roles and responsibilities for managing and maintaining each collaboration tool, and ensure that there is a clear process for requesting and implementing changes or improvements.

4. Provide training and support
- Provide training and support to all team members on how to use each collaboration tool effectively, including how to access, navigate, and troubleshoot the tool.

- Develop user guides, tutorials, or other resources that team members can refer to for guidance and support, and ensure that these resources are easily accessible and up-to-date.
- Encourage team members to share their own tips, tricks, and best practices for using collaboration tools, and create opportunities for peer-to-peer learning and support.

5. Monitor and optimize tool usage
- Regularly monitor and analyze how collaboration tools are being used, including metrics such as adoption rates, usage patterns, and user feedback.
- Identify any areas where collaboration tools are being underutilized, misused, or causing confusion or frustration, and work with the team to identify root causes and develop solutions.
- Continuously optimize and refine the use of collaboration tools based on changing project needs, team dynamics, or external factors, and ensure that all team members are informed and aligned on any changes or updates.

6. Integrate collaboration tools with other systems and processes
- Ensure that collaboration tools are integrated with other project management systems and processes, such as timelines, budgets, or quality assurance, to provide a holistic and seamless collaboration experience.

Use APIs, plugins, or other integration tools to automate data flow and synchronization between collaboration tools and other systems, and ensure that all team members have access to the necessary information and insights.

- Regularly review and update the integration between collaboration tools and other systems to ensure that they remain aligned and effective, and that any issues or inconsistencies are identified and resolved.

Using collaboration tools effectively is critical for ensuring that the project team can work together efficiently and effectively, even when working remotely. However, it's important to remember that collaboration tools are not a silver bullet, and that they require ongoing attention, support, and optimization to be truly effective.

To overcome these challenges, remote project managers can use a variety of strategies, such as:

- Conducting regular check-ins and surveys to assess team members' satisfaction and engagement with collaboration tools, and to identify areas for improvement or additional support.
- Encouraging team members to experiment with and adapt collaboration tools to their own needs and preferences, while still adhering to the overall guidelines and protocols.
- Providing opportunities for team members to share their own experiences and insights on collaboration tools, and to learn from and support each other in using these tools effectively.
- Continuously evaluating and adapting the collaboration tool stack based on changing project needs, team dynamics, or external factors, and ensuring that all team members are informed and aligned on any changes or updates.

Regularly review and update the integration between collaboration tools and other systems to ensure that they remain aligned and effective, and that any issues or inconsistencies are identified and resolved.

Using collaboration tools effectively is critical for ensuring that the project team can work together efficiently and effectively, even when working remotely. However, it's important to remember that collaboration tools are not a silver bullet, and that they require ongoing attention, support, and optimization to be truly effective.

To overcome these challenges, remote project managers can use a variety of strategies, such as:

- Conducting regular check-ins and surveys to assess team members' satisfaction and engagement with collaboration tools, and to identify areas for improvement or additional support.
- Encouraging team members to experiment with and adapt collaboration tools to their own needs and preferences, while still adhering to the overall guidelines and protocols.
- Providing opportunities for team members to share their own experiences and insights on collaboration tools, and to learn from and support each other in using these tools effectively.
- Continuously evaluating and adapting the collaboration tool stack based on changing project needs, team dynamics, or external factors, and ensuring that all team members are informed and aligned on any changes or updates.

By using collaboration tools effectively and efficiently, remote project managers can help their virtual teams work together seamlessly, share information and ideas, and deliver high-quality results that meet or exceed stakeholder expectations.

So if you're a remote project manager, make collaboration tools a priority. Identify collaboration needs and requirements, select the right collaboration tools, establish clear guidelines and protocols, provide training and support, monitor and optimize tool usage, and integrate collaboration tools with other systems and processes. By creating a culture of effective and efficient virtual collaboration, you'll be well-equipped to lead your virtual team to success, no matter how complex or challenging the project may be.

Providing Regular Updates and Feedback

Effective communication is the backbone of any successful project, and this is especially true in a remote setting where team members may be working across different locations, time zones, and cultures. As a remote project manager, it's your responsibility to ensure that team members are kept informed and aligned on project progress, issues, and priorities, and that they receive regular updates and feedback on their work and contributions.

Providing regular updates and feedback involves a combination of proactive communication, active listening, and constructive dialogue. Here are some key steps to follow:

1. Establish a regular cadence of updates
- Determine the appropriate frequency and format for project updates, based on the project timeline, complexity, and stakeholder needs.
- Consider using a variety of update formats, such as status reports, bulletins, newsletters, or dashboards, to cater to different communication preferences and styles.
- Ensure that updates are concise, relevant, and actionable, and that they provide a clear and accurate picture of project progress, issues, and risks.

2. Communicate progress and achievements
- Regularly communicate project progress and achievements to team members and stakeholders, highlighting key milestones, deliverables, and successes.

- Use data and metrics to quantify progress and impact, and provide context and analysis to help team members understand the significance and implications of the achievements.
- Celebrate and recognize individual and team contributions and successes, and ensure that everyone feels valued and appreciated for their work and efforts.

3. Address issues and challenges
- Proactively identify and communicate any issues, challenges, or risks that may impact project progress or success, and ensure that team members are aware of and prepared for these challenges.
- Provide clear and objective information on the nature, scope, and impact of the issues, and engage team members in identifying and evaluating potential solutions and mitigation strategies.
- Ensure that issues and challenges are escalated and addressed in a timely and effective manner, and that team members are kept informed and involved in the resolution process.

4. Provide regular feedback
- Regularly provide feedback to team members on their work, contributions, and performance, using a combination of formal and informal feedback channels and methods.
- Use a balanced and constructive approach to feedback, highlighting both strengths and areas for improvement, and providing specific and actionable guidance and support.

- Encourage team members to seek and provide feedback to each other, and create a culture of continuous learning, growth, and improvement.

5. **Encourage open communication and dialogue**
- Create a safe and inclusive environment where team members feel comfortable and encouraged to share their thoughts, ideas, and concerns, and to engage in open and honest dialogue.
- Use active listening and empathy to understand and validate team members' perspectives and experiences, and to build trust and rapport.
- Encourage team members to ask questions, challenge assumptions, and propose alternative solutions and approaches, and ensure that all voices and perspectives are heard and valued.

6. **Adapt and improve communication over time**
- Regularly solicit feedback from team members and stakeholders on the effectiveness and impact of project updates and feedback, and use this feedback to identify areas for improvement and innovation.
- Experiment with new communication channels, formats, and techniques, and assess their impact and value in enhancing project communication and collaboration.
- Continuously refine and adapt the project communication plan and processes based on changing project needs, team dynamics, and external factors, and ensure that all team members are informed and aligned on any changes or updates.

Providing regular updates and feedback is critical for ensuring that the project team stays informed, aligned, and engaged, even when working remotely. However, it's important to remember that communication is a two-way process, and that team members also have a responsibility to actively seek and provide updates and feedback, and to engage in open and constructive dialogue.

To overcome these challenges, remote project managers can use a variety of strategies, such as:

- Using a variety of communication channels and formats, such as video conferencing, instant messaging, or project management software, to cater to different communication preferences and needs.
- Providing training and support to team members on effective communication and feedback skills, and modeling these skills in their own communication and interactions.
- Creating opportunities for team members to share their own updates and feedback, and to engage in peer-to-peer learning and support.
- Continuously monitoring and evaluating the effectiveness and impact of project communication and feedback, and using data and insights to inform and improve communication strategies and processes.

By providing regular updates and feedback that are timely, relevant, and constructive, remote project managers can help their virtual teams stay informed, aligned, and motivated, and deliver high-quality results that meet or exceed stakeholder expectations.

So if you're a remote project manager, make regular updates and feedback a priority. Establish a regular cadence of updates, communicate progress and achievements, address issues and challenges, provide regular feedback, encourage open communication and dialogue, and adapt and improve communication over time. By creating a culture of transparency, trust, and continuous improvement, you'll be well-equipped to lead your virtual team to success, no matter how complex or challenging the project may be.

Chapter 6
Project Closure and Evaluation

Conducting Project Reviews and Retrospectives

As the project comes to a close, it's important to take the time to reflect on the project journey, celebrate the successes, and identify opportunities for improvement. Conducting project reviews and retrospectives is a key part of this process, and it's an essential responsibility of the remote project manager to ensure that these activities are planned, facilitated, and followed up on effectively.

Project reviews and retrospectives are structured meetings or workshops that bring together the project team, stakeholders, and other relevant parties to evaluate the project outcomes, processes, and experiences, and to identify lessons learned and best practices that can be applied to future projects. Here are some key steps to follow when conducting project reviews and retrospectives:

1. Plan and prepare
- Determine the scope, objectives, and format of the project review or retrospective, based on the project complexity, timeline, and stakeholder needs.
- Identify and invite the appropriate participants, ensuring that all relevant perspectives and experiences are represented and valued.
- Develop a clear agenda and timeline for the review or retrospective, and communicate this to all participants in advance.

- Gather and organize relevant data, documents, and artifacts that will be used to inform and support the review or retrospective, such as project plans, status reports, deliverables, and feedback.

2. Set the stage
- Begin the review or retrospective by setting a positive and constructive tone, and by reinforcing the purpose and expectations for the meeting.
- Use icebreakers or other activities to build rapport and trust among participants, and to create a safe and inclusive environment for open and honest dialogue.
- Establish ground rules and norms for participation and communication, and ensure that all participants understand and agree to these rules.

3. Review project outcomes and deliverables
- Review and evaluate the project outcomes and deliverables against the original project goals, objectives, and requirements, and assess the extent to which these were met or exceeded.
- Use data and metrics to quantify the project impact and value, and provide context and analysis to help participants understand the significance and implications of the outcomes.
- Identify and celebrate the key successes and achievements of the project, and recognize the individual and team contributions that made these possible.

4. Reflect on project processes and experiences
- Reflect on the project processes, tools, and methods that were used, and evaluate their effectiveness and efficiency in supporting project delivery and collaboration.
- Discuss the project experiences and challenges that were encountered, and explore the root causes and impacts of these experiences.
- Identify the key lessons learned and best practices that emerged from the project, and discuss how these can be captured, shared, and applied to future projects.

5. Generate insights and recommendations
- Use structured brainstorming, prioritization, and analysis techniques to generate insights and recommendations for improving project processes, tools, and methods.
- Encourage participants to think creatively and critically about potential solutions and innovations, and to challenge assumptions and status quo approaches.
- Document and prioritize the key insights and recommendations, and develop an action plan for implementing and following up on these recommendations.

6. Close and follow up
- Close the review or retrospective by summarizing the key outcomes, insights, and recommendations, and by reinforcing the value and importance of the activity.
- Thank and recognize all participants for their contributions and engagement, and ensure that they feel heard, valued, and appreciated.

- Distribute the review or retrospective documentation to all relevant parties, and ensure that the insights and recommendations are communicated and acted upon in a timely and effective manner.

Conducting project reviews and retrospectives is critical for ensuring that the project team and stakeholders have an opportunity to reflect on and learn from the project experience, and to identify opportunities for continuous improvement and innovation. However, it's important to remember that reviews and retrospectives are not a one-time event, but an ongoing process that requires regular attention and follow-up.

To overcome these challenges, remote project managers can use a variety of strategies, such as:

- Using virtual collaboration tools and techniques, such as video conferencing, screen sharing, and online whiteboards, to facilitate remote participation and engagement in reviews and retrospectives.
- Providing training and support to participants on effective communication, feedback, and problem-solving skills, and modeling these skills in their own facilitation and leadership.
- Creating a culture of continuous learning and improvement, where insights and recommendations from reviews and retrospectives are valued, shared, and acted upon in a timely and effective manner.

- Continuously monitoring and evaluating the effectiveness and impact of project reviews and retrospectives, and using data and insights to inform and improve the review and retrospective processes and outcomes.

By conducting project reviews and retrospectives that are well-planned, facilitated, and followed up on, remote project managers can help their virtual teams reflect on and learn from the project experience, celebrate successes, and identify opportunities for continuous improvement and innovation.

So if you're a remote project manager, make project reviews and retrospectives a priority. Plan and prepare, set the stage, review project outcomes and deliverables, reflect on project processes and experiences, generate insights and recommendations, and close and follow up. By creating a culture of reflection, learning, and growth, you'll be well-equipped to lead your virtual team to success, both in the current project and in future endeavors.

Documenting Lessons Learned

One of the most valuable outcomes of conducting project reviews and retrospectives is the identification and documentation of lessons learned. Lessons learned are the key insights, knowledge, and experiences that are gained from a project, and that can be used to inform and improve future projects and practices. As a remote project manager, it's your responsibility to ensure that lessons learned are captured, shared, and applied effectively, so that the project team and the organization as a whole can benefit from the collective wisdom and expertise of the project.

Documenting lessons learned involves a structured and systematic process of gathering, organizing, and communicating the insights and recommendations that emerge from project reviews and retrospectives. Here are some key steps to follow when documenting lessons learned:

1. **Identify and prioritize lessons learned**
   - During project reviews and retrospectives, actively listen for and identify the key lessons learned that emerge from the discussions and reflections.
   - Use structured techniques, such as affinity mapping or impact/effort matrices, to organize and prioritize the lessons learned based on their relevance, importance, and feasibility.
   - Ensure that the lessons learned are specific, actionable, and supported by evidence and examples from the project experience.

2. Capture and document lessons learned
Use a consistent and standardized format and template for documenting lessons learned, such as a lessons learned log or report.
- For each lesson learned, provide a clear and concise description of the insight or recommendation, along with the context, rationale, and implications of the lesson.
- Use rich and engaging formats, such as stories, case studies, or videos, to bring the lessons learned to life and make them more memorable and impactful.
- Ensure that the lessons learned documentation is complete, accurate, and up-to-date, and that it reflects the diverse perspectives and experiences of the project team and stakeholders.

3. Share and communicate lessons learned
- Develop a communication plan for sharing and disseminating the lessons learned documentation to all relevant parties, such as project team members, stakeholders, and other project managers and teams.
- Use a variety of communication channels and formats, such as email, newsletters, webinars, or knowledge management systems, to reach and engage different audiences and learning styles.
- Encourage feedback, discussion, and dialogue around the lessons learned, and create opportunities for peer-to-peer learning and knowledge sharing.
- Ensure that the lessons learned are easily accessible, searchable, and reusable, and that they are integrated into the organization's knowledge management and learning systems.

4. Apply and integrate lessons learned
- Work with project team members, stakeholders, and other relevant parties to identify opportunities for applying and integrating the lessons learned into current and future projects and practices.
- Use the lessons learned to inform and improve project planning, execution, and monitoring processes, and to identify and mitigate potential risks and issues.
- Encourage and support project team members to experiment with and adapt the lessons learned to their own contexts and needs, and to share their experiences and insights with others.
- Monitor and evaluate the impact and effectiveness of the lessons learned application and integration, and use this feedback to refine and improve the lessons learned documentation and processes.

5. Continuously update and improve lessons learned
- Treat lessons learned documentation as a living and evolving resource, and ensure that it is regularly reviewed, updated, and improved based on new insights, experiences, and feedback.
- Encourage and empower project team members and stakeholders to contribute to and co-create the lessons learned documentation, and to take ownership and responsibility for its ongoing development and improvement.
- Use data and analytics to track and measure the usage, impact, and value of the lessons learned documentation, and to identify areas for optimization and innovation.

- Celebrate and recognize the contributions and achievements of project team members and stakeholders in capturing, sharing, and applying lessons learned, and create a culture of continuous learning and improvement.

Documenting lessons learned is a critical component of effective project management, and it's especially important in a remote setting where project team members and stakeholders may be dispersed and disconnected. By capturing, sharing, and applying the collective wisdom and expertise of the project, remote project managers can help their virtual teams to learn from the past, improve the present, and prepare for the future.

To overcome the challenges of documenting lessons learned in a remote setting, remote project managers can use a variety of strategies, such as:
- Using collaborative documentation tools and platforms, such as wikis, blogs, or knowledge management systems, to facilitate remote contribution, review, and feedback on lessons learned documentation.
- Providing training and support to project team members and stakeholders on effective documentation, communication, and knowledge sharing skills, and modeling these skills in their own practices and behaviors.
- Creating a culture of transparency, trust, and psychological safety, where project team members and stakeholders feel comfortable and motivated to share their insights, experiences, and recommendations, and to engage in open and constructive dialogue and debate.

- Continuously monitoring and evaluating the effectiveness and impact of lessons learned documentation and processes, and using data and insights to inform and improve the lessons learned practices and outcomes.

By documenting lessons learned effectively and efficiently, remote project managers can help their virtual teams to capture, share, and apply the valuable insights and knowledge that emerge from project experiences, and to create a culture of continuous learning, improvement, and innovation.

So if you're a remote project manager, make documenting lessons learned a priority. Identify and prioritize lessons learned, capture and document lessons learned, share and communicate lessons learned, apply and integrate lessons learned, and continuously update and improve lessons learned. By creating a culture of knowledge sharing, collaboration, and growth, you'll be well-equipped to lead your virtual team to success, both in the current project and in future endeavors.

Celebrating Project Successes

As a project comes to a close, it's important to take the time to celebrate the successes and achievements of the project team. Celebrating project successes is not just a nice-to-have or an afterthought, but a critical component of effective project management. It's an opportunity to recognize and appreciate the hard work, dedication, and contributions of the project team members, to reinforce the value and impact of the project outcomes, and to create a positive and motivating environment for future projects and collaborations.

As a remote project manager, it's your responsibility to ensure that project successes are celebrated in a meaningful, inclusive, and impactful way, even when the project team is dispersed and disconnected. Here are some key steps to follow when celebrating project successes:

1. **Identify and communicate project successes**
   - Throughout the project lifecycle, actively look for and identify the key successes and achievements of the project team, such as meeting project milestones, delivering high-quality deliverables, or receiving positive feedback from stakeholders.
   - Communicate project successes regularly and consistently to the project team, stakeholders, and the wider organization, using a variety of channels and formats, such as email, newsletters, social media, or virtual events.

- Ensure that project successes are framed and communicated in a way that is meaningful, relevant, and inspiring to different audiences and perspectives.

2. Recognize and appreciate individual and team contributions

- Take the time to recognize and appreciate the individual and team contributions that made project successes possible, such as going above and beyond, demonstrating leadership and initiative, or overcoming challenges and obstacles.
- Use a variety of recognition and appreciation methods, such as public acknowledgments, personal thank-you notes, or small tokens of appreciation, to show gratitude and respect for the project team members' efforts and achievements.
- Ensure that recognition and appreciation are given in a fair, equitable, and inclusive way, and that they reflect the diverse contributions and perspectives of the project team.

3. Celebrate project successes in a meaningful and memorable way

- Plan and execute a project celebration event or activity that is meaningful, memorable, and enjoyable for the project team and stakeholders, such as a virtual party, a team outing, or a special recognition ceremony.
- Use the project celebration as an opportunity to reflect on and reinforce the key lessons learned, best practices, and achievements of the project, and to create a sense of closure and accomplishment for the project team.

- Ensure that the project celebration is inclusive, accessible, and engaging for all project team members and stakeholders, regardless of their location, timezone, or cultural background.

4. Share project successes with the wider organization and community

- Share project successes and celebrations with the wider organization and community, such as other project teams, departments, or external partners and customers, to create a sense of pride, inspiration, and connection.
- Use project successes and celebrations as an opportunity to showcase the value and impact of the project team's work, and to build relationships and collaborations with other stakeholders and influencers.
- Ensure that project successes and celebrations are shared in a way that is respectful, professional, and aligned with the organization's values and goals.

5. Leverage project successes for continuous improvement and growth

- Use project successes and celebrations as a springboard for continuous improvement and growth, both for the project team and for the wider organization.
- Encourage and support project team members to reflect on and apply the lessons learned and best practices from the project to their own work and development, and to share their insights and experiences with others.
- Use project successes and celebrations to identify and pursue new opportunities for innovation, collaboration, and value creation, and to position the project team and the organization for future success.

Celebrating project successes is a powerful way to create a positive, motivated, and engaged project team, and to build a culture of recognition, appreciation, and continuous improvement. By taking the time to identify, communicate, recognize, celebrate, share, and leverage project successes, remote project managers can help their virtual teams to feel valued, connected, and inspired, even when they are working remotely and independently.

To overcome the challenges of celebrating project successes in a remote setting, remote project managers can use a variety of strategies, such as:

- Using virtual celebration tools and platforms, such as video conferencing, virtual reality, or online games and activities, to create engaging and interactive celebration experiences for the project team and stakeholders.
- Providing resources and support for project team members to plan and execute their own mini-celebrations and recognitions, such as virtual coffee chats, peer-to-peer appreciations, or personal development activities.
- Creating a culture of gratitude, recognition, and celebration, where project successes and contributions are regularly acknowledged and appreciated, and where everyone feels empowered and motivated to celebrate and share their own and others' achievements.
- Continuously monitoring and evaluating the effectiveness and impact of project success celebrations, and using data and insights to inform and improve the celebration practices and outcomes.

Transitioning to New Projects

As one project comes to a close, it's important for project managers to start thinking about transitioning to new projects. This transition period can be both exciting and challenging, as it involves wrapping up the current project, reflecting on lessons learned, and preparing for the new project ahead. As a remote project manager, it's your responsibility to ensure that the transition to new projects is smooth, efficient, and effective, and that the project team is well-prepared and supported throughout the process.

Here are some key steps to follow when transitioning to new projects:

1. **Conduct a project closeout and evaluation**
   - Before transitioning to a new project, take the time to conduct a thorough project closeout and evaluation process for the current project, as discussed in the previous sections on conducting project reviews and retrospectives and documenting lessons learned.
   - Use the project closeout and evaluation process to reflect on and capture the key successes, challenges, and lessons learned from the current project, and to identify areas for improvement and growth for future projects.
   - Ensure that all project deliverables, documentation, and assets are properly archived, stored, and transferred to the appropriate stakeholders and teams.

2. Communicate the transition to the project team and stakeholders

- Communicate the transition to new projects to the project team and stakeholders in a clear, transparent, and timely manner, using a variety of channels and formats, such as email, meetings, or announcements.
- Provide the project team and stakeholders with an overview of the new project, including the project goals, scope, timeline, and roles and responsibilities, and address any questions or concerns they may have.
- Ensure that the project team and stakeholders understand the implications and expectations of the transition, such as changes in project assignments, timelines, or communication channels.

3. Assess and align the project team's skills and resources

- Assess the project team's skills, experience, and availability for the new project, and identify any gaps or development needs that need to be addressed.
- Work with the project team members to align their skills and interests with the new project requirements and opportunities, and to identify areas for growth and development.
- Ensure that the project team has the necessary resources, tools, and support to successfully transition to and execute the new project, such as training, mentoring, or access to subject matter experts.

4. **Plan and prepare for the new project**
   - Work with the project team and stakeholders to plan and prepare for the new project, using the lessons learned and best practices from the previous project as a foundation.
   - Develop a project charter, plan, and timeline for the new project, and ensure that all project team members and stakeholders are aligned and committed to the project goals and expectations.
   - Identify and mitigate any potential risks or challenges that may impact the new project, such as resource constraints, dependencies, or external factors, and develop contingency plans as needed.

5. **Foster a culture of continuous learning and improvement**
   - Use the transition to new projects as an opportunity to foster a culture of continuous learning and improvement, both for the project team and for the wider organization.
   - Encourage and support project team members to reflect on and apply the lessons learned and best practices from the previous project to the new project, and to share their insights and experiences with others.
   - Create opportunities for cross-project collaboration and knowledge sharing, such as communities of practice, mentoring programs, or innovation labs, to leverage the collective wisdom and expertise of the organization.

Transitioning to new projects can be a complex and challenging process, especially in a remote setting where project team members and stakeholders may be dispersed and disconnected. However, by following a structured and proactive approach, remote project managers can help their virtual teams to navigate the transition successfully and to set themselves up for success in the new project.

To overcome the challenges of transitioning to new projects in a remote setting, remote project managers can use a variety of strategies, such as:

- Using virtual collaboration tools and platforms, such as project management software, knowledge management systems, or communication tools, to facilitate remote planning, coordination, and knowledge sharing for the new project.
- Providing training and support for project team members to develop the skills and competencies needed for the new project, such as technical skills, communication skills, or leadership skills, and to adapt to the new project requirements and expectations.
- Creating a culture of adaptability, resilience, and growth, where project team members feel empowered and supported to take on new challenges and opportunities, and to learn and grow from their experiences.
- Continuously monitoring and evaluating the effectiveness and impact of the transition process, and using data and insights to inform and improve the transition practices and outcomes.

By transitioning to new projects effectively and efficiently, remote project managers can help their virtual teams to build on the successes and lessons learned from previous projects, to adapt to new challenges and opportunities, and to create value and impact for the organization and its stakeholders.

So if you're a remote project manager, make transitioning to new projects a priority. Conduct a project closeout and evaluation, communicate the transition to the project team and stakeholders, assess and align the project team's skills and resources, plan and prepare for the new project, and foster a culture of continuous learning and improvement. By creating a culture of adaptability, resilience, and growth, you'll be well-equipped to lead your virtual team to success, both in the current project and in future endeavors.

Part III
Leading and Empowering Virtual Teams

Chapter 7
Building Trust and Rapport
Fostering Open Communication

In a remote project setting, building trust and rapport among team members is essential for creating a positive and productive work environment. When team members trust each other and feel comfortable communicating openly, they are more likely to collaborate effectively, share ideas and knowledge, and work together towards common goals. As a remote project manager, it's your responsibility to foster open communication and build trust and rapport among your virtual team members.

Here are some key strategies for fostering open communication and building trust and rapport in a remote project team:

1. **Establish clear communication channels and norms**
   - Determine the primary communication channels and norms for the project team, such as email, instant messaging, video conferencing, or project management software, and ensure that all team members are aware of and comfortable with using these channels.

- Set clear expectations for communication frequency, response times, and etiquette, such as using professional language, avoiding interruptions, or respecting time zone differences.
- Encourage team members to communicate regularly and proactively, and to share updates, progress, and challenges in a timely and transparent manner.

2. Create opportunities for informal and social interaction
- In addition to formal project communication, create opportunities for team members to interact informally and socially, such as virtual coffee chats, team-building activities, or interest groups.
- Use these informal interactions to get to know team members on a personal level, to learn about their interests, hobbies, and backgrounds, and to build rapport and trust.
- Encourage team members to share photos, videos, or stories from their personal lives, and to celebrate milestones and achievements together, such as birthdays, work anniversaries, or project successes.

3. Model and encourage active listening and empathy
- As a project manager, model active listening and empathy in your own communication with team members, by giving them your full attention, asking questions, and seeking to understand their perspectives and needs.
- Encourage team members to practice active listening and empathy with each other, by avoiding interruptions, asking clarifying questions, and acknowledging and validating each other's feelings and experiences.

- Create a safe and supportive environment where team members feel comfortable expressing their thoughts, ideas, and concerns, and where they know they will be heard and respected.

4. Foster a culture of transparency and accountability
- Create a culture of transparency and accountability within the project team, by sharing information openly and honestly, admitting mistakes and challenges, and taking responsibility for actions and outcomes.
- Encourage team members to be transparent about their work progress, challenges, and needs, and to hold each other accountable for meeting project goals and commitments.
- Celebrate successes and learn from failures together as a team, and use these experiences to build trust, resilience, and continuous improvement.

5. Provide feedback and recognition regularly
- Provide regular feedback and recognition to team members, both individually and as a team, to acknowledge their contributions, progress, and achievements.
- Use a variety of feedback and recognition methods, such as one-on-one check-ins, team meetings, or public acknowledgments, to tailor your approach to each team member's preferences and needs.
- Encourage team members to provide feedback and recognition to each other, and to celebrate each other's successes and milestones.

6. Address conflicts and issues proactively and constructively
- When conflicts or issues arise within the project team, address them proactively and constructively, by bringing the parties together to discuss the situation openly and respectfully.
- Use active listening, empathy, and problem-solving skills to understand the root causes of the conflict or issue, and to brainstorm potential solutions and compromises.
- Encourage team members to take ownership of their actions and to work together to resolve conflicts and issues in a way that strengthens trust and rapport, rather than undermining it.

Fostering open communication and building trust and rapport among virtual team members requires intentional and ongoing effort from the project manager and the entire team. It involves creating a supportive and inclusive team culture, modeling and encouraging positive communication behaviors, and addressing conflicts and issues in a timely and constructive manner.

To overcome the challenges of fostering open communication and building trust and rapport in a remote setting, project managers can use a variety of strategies, such as:
- Using virtual team-building activities and icebreakers to create opportunities for informal interaction and personal connection among team members.
- Leveraging video conferencing and other rich media communication tools to enhance nonverbal cues and emotional connection among team members.

- Providing training and coaching on communication, active listening, and conflict resolution skills to help team members communicate more effectively and build stronger relationships.
- Continuously monitoring and assessing the team's communication and trust levels, and using feedback and data to identify areas for improvement and adjust strategies accordingly.

By fostering open communication and building trust and rapport among virtual team members, remote project managers can create a positive and productive team environment that enables collaboration, innovation, and success. When team members feel safe, supported, and connected to each other, they are more likely to bring their best selves to the project and to work together towards common goals.

So if you're a remote project manager, make building trust and rapport a top priority. Establish clear communication channels and norms, create opportunities for informal and social interaction, model and encourage active listening and empathy, foster a culture of transparency and accountability, provide feedback and recognition regularly, and address conflicts and issues proactively and constructively. By investing in your team's relationships and communication skills, you'll be well-equipped to lead and empower your virtual team to achieve great things together.

Encouraging Team Bonding and Socializing

In a remote project setting, encouraging team bonding and socializing is crucial for building a strong and cohesive team culture. When team members have opportunities to connect with each other on a personal level, they are more likely to trust, support, and collaborate with each other effectively. As a remote project manager, it's your responsibility to create and facilitate opportunities for team bonding and socializing, even when team members are not physically together.

Here are some key strategies for encouraging team bonding and socializing in a remote project team:

1. **Schedule regular team-building activities and events**
   - Plan and schedule regular team-building activities and events, such as virtual happy hours, game nights, or skill-sharing sessions, to provide opportunities for team members to interact and have fun together.
   - Use a variety of team-building formats and themes, such as icebreakers, trivia, storytelling, or creative challenges, to cater to different interests and preferences among team members.
   - Encourage team members to take turns leading or organizing team-building activities, to promote ownership and engagement.

2. **Create shared spaces and channels for casual conversation**
   - Create shared virtual spaces and channels, such as chat rooms, forums, or social media groups, where team members can engage in casual conversation and share personal updates, photos, or stories.
   - Encourage team members to use these spaces and channels regularly, and to initiate and participate in conversations beyond work-related topics.
   - Model and promote a friendly, inclusive, and respectful tone in these spaces and channels, and address any inappropriate or offensive behavior promptly and constructively.

3. **Celebrate milestones and achievements together**
   - Make a point of celebrating team and individual milestones and achievements, such as project successes, work anniversaries, or personal accomplishments, to foster a sense of pride and belonging among team members.
   - Use virtual celebration tools and techniques, such as e-cards, video montages, or online gift-giving, to make these celebrations memorable and meaningful.
   - Encourage team members to share their own milestones and achievements, and to congratulate and support each other's successes.

4. **Encourage informal peer-to-peer interaction and mentoring**
   - Encourage team members to connect and interact with each other informally, outside of scheduled meetings and events, to build rapport and learn from each other.

- Create opportunities for peer-to-peer mentoring and knowledge-sharing, such as pairing experienced team members with newer ones, or creating interest-based learning groups.
- Provide resources and support for team members to initiate and facilitate their own informal interactions and mentoring relationships, such as communication tools, meeting agendas, or discussion guides.

5. **Foster a culture of inclusivity and diversity**
- Foster a culture of inclusivity and diversity within the project team, by welcoming and valuing different perspectives, backgrounds, and communication styles among team members.
- Encourage team members to share and learn about each other's cultures, traditions, and experiences, and to celebrate and appreciate the richness and diversity of the team.
- Address any instances of bias, discrimination, or exclusion promptly and constructively, and provide training and resources on diversity, equity, and inclusion to help team members build cultural competence and empathy.

6. **Lead by example and participate actively**
- As a project manager, lead by example by participating actively and enthusiastically in team bonding and socializing activities and conversations.
- Share your own personal stories, interests, and experiences with the team, and show genuine interest and curiosity in learning about others.

- Encourage and support other team members to take on leadership roles in team bonding and socializing, and provide feedback and recognition for their efforts.

Encouraging team bonding and socializing in a remote project setting requires creativity, intentionality, and consistency from the project manager and the entire team. It involves creating a variety of opportunities and channels for personal connection and interaction, fostering a culture of inclusivity and diversity, and leading by example and participation.

To overcome the challenges of encouraging team bonding and socializing in a remote setting, project managers can use a variety of strategies, such as:

- Leveraging virtual team-building platforms and tools, such as online escape rooms, virtual reality experiences, or interactive games, to create engaging and immersive bonding experiences.
- Providing resources and budgets for team members to organize and participate in virtual social events and activities, such as cooking classes, book clubs, or fitness challenges.
- Encouraging team members to share photos, videos, and stories from their personal lives and interests, and creating virtual spaces and channels for these sharing and conversations.
- Continuously soliciting feedback and ideas from team members on how to improve and enhance team bonding and socializing, and using this input to refine and adapt strategies over time.

By encouraging team bonding and socializing in a remote project setting, project managers can create a strong and supportive team culture that enhances trust, collaboration, and engagement among team members. When team members feel personally connected and invested in each other's well-being and success, they are more likely to go above and beyond in their work and to weather challenges and setbacks together.

So if you're a remote project manager, make team bonding and socializing a priority. Schedule regular team-building activities and events, create shared spaces and channels for casual conversation, celebrate milestones and achievements together, encourage informal peer-to-peer interaction and mentoring, foster a culture of inclusivity and diversity, and lead by example and participate actively. By investing in your team's personal relationships and connections, you'll be well-equipped to build a high-performing and resilient virtual team that can achieve great things together.

Demonstrating Empathy and Emotional Intelligence

In a remote project setting, demonstrating empathy and emotional intelligence is essential for building trust, rapport, and effective communication among team members. When team members feel understood, supported, and valued by their project manager and colleagues, they are more likely to be engaged, motivated, and resilient in the face of challenges and changes. As a remote project manager, it's your responsibility to model and promote empathy and emotional intelligence in your own leadership style and in your team's interactions.

Here are some key strategies for demonstrating empathy and emotional intelligence in a remote project setting:

1. Practice active listening and understanding
- When communicating with team members, practice active listening by giving them your full attention, avoiding distractions or multitasking, and focusing on understanding their perspectives and needs.
- Use paraphrasing, reflective statements, and clarifying questions to show that you are listening and to ensure that you have accurately understood what team members are saying.
- Avoid making assumptions or judgments about team members' intentions or feelings, and instead seek to understand their underlying motivations and concerns.

2. **Acknowledge and validate emotions and experiences**
   - When team members express emotions or share personal experiences, acknowledge and validate their feelings and perspectives, even if you don't fully agree or understand them.
   - Use empathetic statements and body language, such as nodding, smiling, or expressing concern, to show that you are attuned to and supportive of team members' emotional states.
   - Avoid minimizing, dismissing, or trying to fix team members' emotions or experiences, and instead focus on providing a safe and supportive space for them to express themselves.

3. Adapt your communication style to individual preferences and needs
   - Recognize that different team members may have different communication styles, preferences, and needs, based on their personality, culture, or work style.
   - Adapt your own communication style and approach to match team members' preferences and needs, such as using more visual or written communication for some team members, or providing more frequent check-ins or feedback for others.
   - Encourage team members to share their communication preferences and needs with you and with each other, and to be open and flexible in adapting to different styles and approaches.

4. Show genuine interest and care for team members' well-being
- Beyond work-related conversations, show genuine interest and care for team members' personal well-being, such as their health, family, or hobbies.
- Take time to check in with team members regularly, both individually and as a group, to see how they are doing and to offer support or resources as needed.
- Encourage team members to prioritize their own self-care and work-life balance, and model these behaviors yourself by setting boundaries, taking breaks, and sharing your own personal interests and experiences.

5. Address conflicts and challenges with empathy and skill
- When conflicts or challenges arise within the team, approach them with empathy and emotional intelligence, seeking to understand all perspectives and find mutually beneficial solutions.
- Use active listening, open-ended questions, and collaborative problem-solving techniques to facilitate constructive dialogue and resolution among team members.
- Provide coaching and support to help team members develop their own empathy and emotional intelligence skills, such as self-awareness, self-regulation, and social awareness.

6. Celebrate and appreciate the unique strengths and contributions of each team member
- Recognize and celebrate the unique strengths, talents, and contributions of each team member, and help them see how their individual qualities contribute to the success of the team and the project.
- Provide specific, personalized, and timely appreciation and recognition to team members, both privately and publicly, to reinforce their value and importance to the team.
- Encourage team members to appreciate and celebrate each other's strengths and contributions, and create opportunities for peer recognition and feedback.

Demonstrating empathy and emotional intelligence in a remote project setting requires intentional and consistent effort from the project manager and the entire team. It involves developing and practicing skills such as active listening, emotional awareness, adaptability, and conflict resolution, and creating a team culture that values and supports these behaviors.

To overcome the challenges of demonstrating empathy and emotional intelligence in a remote setting, project managers can use a variety of strategies, such as:

- Using video conferencing and other rich media communication tools to enhance nonverbal cues and emotional connection among team members.

- Providing training and resources on emotional intelligence, active listening, and conflict resolution skills to help team members develop and practice these competencies.
- Encouraging team members to share their own experiences and perspectives on empathy and emotional intelligence, and to provide feedback and support to each other in developing these skills.
- Continuously monitoring and assessing the team's emotional climate and dynamics, and using this information to identify areas for improvement and to adjust leadership and communication strategies accordingly.

By demonstrating empathy and emotional intelligence in a remote project setting, project managers can create a team environment that is supportive, inclusive, and emotionally intelligent. When team members feel understood, valued, and cared for by their project manager and colleagues, they are more likely to be engaged, committed, and high-performing, even in the face of challenges and uncertainties.

So if you're a remote project manager, make empathy and emotional intelligence a core part of your leadership style and team culture. Practice active listening and understanding, acknowledge and validate emotions and experiences, adapt your communication style to individual preferences and needs, show genuine interest and care for team members' well-being, address conflicts and challenges with empathy and skill, and celebrate and appreciate the unique strengths and contributions of each team member.

By investing in your own and your team's emotional intelligence and empathy skills, you'll be well-equipped to build a remote team that is resilient, cohesive, and successful.

Leading by Example

In a remote project setting, leading by example is one of the most powerful ways for project managers to inspire, motivate, and guide their teams towards success. When project managers consistently model the behaviors, values, and work ethic that they expect from their team members, they create a culture of accountability, trust, and high performance. As a remote project manager, it's your responsibility to set the tone and standard for your team through your own actions and attitudes.

Here are some key strategies for leading by example in a remote project setting:

1. **Demonstrate strong work ethic and reliability**
   - Consistently show up on time and prepared for meetings, events, and deadlines, and follow through on your commitments and responsibilities.
   - Maintain a high standard of quality and professionalism in your own work, and take ownership and accountability for your mistakes and areas for improvement.
   - Communicate proactively and transparently about your availability, progress, and challenges, and avoid making excuses or blaming others for setbacks or issues.

2. **Model effective communication and collaboration**
   - Use clear, concise, and respectful language in all your communication with team members, stakeholders, and customers, and avoid jargon, sarcasm, or ambiguity.

- Listen actively and empathetically to others' perspectives and ideas, and seek to understand before being understood.
- Collaborate openly and generously with team members and stakeholders, sharing information, resources, and credit, and avoiding silos, competition, or politics.

3. **Demonstrate adaptability and resilience**
   - Embrace change and uncertainty as opportunities for learning and growth, and model a positive and proactive attitude towards challenges and setbacks.
   - Be open to feedback, constructive criticism, and new ideas, and demonstrate a willingness to learn and adapt your approach based on input from others.
   - Show resilience and perseverance in the face of obstacles and failures, and encourage your team to do the same by framing challenges as opportunities for innovation and improvement.

4. **Model work-life balance and self-care**
   - Set and maintain healthy boundaries between work and personal life, and avoid overworking, burnout, or neglecting your own well-being.
   - Take regular breaks, vacations, and time off to recharge and pursue personal interests and relationships, and encourage your team to do the same.
   - Model self-care practices such as exercise, mindfulness, hobbies, and social connections, and create a team culture that values and supports these practices.

5. Demonstrate integrity and ethical behavior
- Act with honesty, transparency, and fairness in all your dealings with team members, stakeholders, and customers, and avoid any actions or decisions that could be perceived as unethical or self-serving.
- Hold yourself and others accountable to high standards of integrity and professionalism, and address any breaches or concerns promptly and constructively.
- Model a commitment to diversity, equity, and inclusion in your hiring, promotion, and team-building practices, and create a team culture that values and celebrates differences and perspectives.

6. Lead with empathy and emotional intelligence
- Show genuine care, concern, and understanding for your team members' experiences, emotions, and needs, and create a safe and supportive environment for them to express themselves.
- Use active listening, reflective questioning, and nonverbal cues to build rapport, trust, and connection with your team members, even in a remote setting.
- Model vulnerability, humility, and authenticity in your own communication and behavior, and encourage your team to do the same by sharing your own challenges, mistakes, and growth opportunities.

Leading by example in a remote project setting requires consistency, intentionality, and self-awareness from project managers. It involves aligning your own actions and attitudes with the values and behaviors that you expect from your team, and continuously seeking feedback and improvement in your own leadership style and practices.

To overcome the challenges of leading by example in a remote setting, project managers can use a variety of strategies, such as:

- Scheduling regular one-on-one check-ins with team members to provide individualized feedback, coaching, and support, and to model active listening and empathy.
- Creating opportunities for team members to provide anonymous feedback and suggestions on your leadership style and practices, and using this input to identify areas for improvement and growth.
- Sharing your own learning and development goals and progress with your team, and inviting them to hold you accountable and provide support and feedback along the way.
- Celebrating and recognizing team members who demonstrate exemplary behaviors and values, and using their examples to reinforce and amplify the desired team culture and norms.

By leading by example in a remote project setting, project managers can create a team culture of trust, accountability, and high performance, even in the face of challenges and uncertainties. When team members see their project manager consistently modeling the behaviors and values that they expect from others, they are more likely to follow suit and contribute their best efforts and ideas to the project.

Chapter 8
Strategies for Effective Team Collaboration

Defining Clear Roles and Responsibilities

In a remote project setting, effective team collaboration is essential for achieving project goals, delivering high-quality results, and fostering a positive team culture. When team members have a clear understanding of their roles, responsibilities, and expectations, they are more likely to work together efficiently, avoid duplication or gaps in work, and hold each other accountable for their contributions. As a remote project manager, it's your responsibility to define and communicate clear roles and responsibilities for your team, and to create a framework for effective collaboration and coordination.

Here are some key strategies for defining clear roles and responsibilities and promoting effective team collaboration in a remote project setting:

1. **Clarify project goals, deliverables, and timeline**
   - Ensure that all team members have a clear and shared understanding of the project's overall goals, scope, deliverables, and timeline, and how their individual roles and responsibilities contribute to these outcomes.
   - Break down the project into smaller, manageable tasks and milestones, and assign clear owners and due dates for each task, using a project management tool or template.

- Communicate any changes or updates to the project goals, deliverables, or timeline promptly and transparently, and seek input and buy-in from team members on any significant revisions.

2. Define roles and responsibilities using a RACI matrix
- Use a RACI (Responsible, Accountable, Consulted, Informed) matrix or similar tool to clearly define and document the roles and responsibilities of each team member for each project task or deliverable.
- Ensure that each task or deliverable has a single owner who is responsible for completing the work, and a single person who is accountable for ensuring that the work meets the required standards and outcomes.
- Identify any team members who need to be consulted or informed about each task or deliverable, and establish clear communication channels and protocols for keeping them in the loop.

3. Align roles and responsibilities with skills, strengths, and interests
- When assigning roles and responsibilities, consider each team member's unique skills, strengths, and interests, and seek to match them with tasks and deliverables that play to their abilities and passions.
- Encourage team members to share their own preferences and goals for their roles and responsibilities, and be open to adjusting assignments based on their input and feedback.

- Provide opportunities for team members to learn and grow in their roles, by offering training, mentoring, or stretch assignments that challenge them to develop new skills and expertise.

4. Foster a culture of collaboration and shared ownership
- Encourage team members to collaborate and support each other in their roles and responsibilities, rather than working in silos or competing for credit or resources.
- Create opportunities for team members to share their work, provide feedback and input on each other's deliverables, and celebrate each other's successes and milestones.
- Model a culture of shared ownership and accountability, where everyone takes responsibility for the overall success of the project, not just their individual tasks or deliverables.

5. Establish clear communication and coordination protocols
- Establish clear and consistent communication and coordination protocols for the team, such as regular status meetings, progress reports, or collaboration tools, to ensure that everyone is aligned and informed about each other's work and progress.
- Encourage team members to proactively communicate and escalate any issues, risks, or dependencies that may impact their roles or responsibilities, and work together to identify and implement solutions or workarounds.

- Use visual tools such as Kanban boards, Gantt charts, or dashboards to provide a shared view of the project's progress, priorities, and dependencies, and to facilitate collaboration and coordination among team members.

6. Continuously monitor and adjust roles and responsibilities
- Regularly review and assess the effectiveness and clarity of the team's roles and responsibilities, and seek feedback and input from team members on any areas for improvement or clarification.
- Be open to adjusting roles and responsibilities as the project evolves and new challenges or opportunities arise, and involve team members in the decision-making process for any significant changes.
- Celebrate and recognize team members who demonstrate exceptional collaboration, ownership, and results in their roles and responsibilities, and use their examples to reinforce and amplify the desired team culture and norms.

Defining clear roles and responsibilities and promoting effective team collaboration in a remote project setting requires intentional and ongoing effort from project managers and team members alike. It involves creating a shared understanding of the project goals and deliverables, using tools and frameworks to clarify and document roles and responsibilities, fostering a culture of collaboration and shared ownership, establishing clear communication and coordination protocols, and continuously monitoring and adjusting roles and responsibilities as needed.

To overcome the challenges of defining clear roles and responsibilities and promoting effective team collaboration in a remote setting, project managers can use a variety of strategies, such as:

- Using online collaboration tools and platforms, such as project management software, shared documents, or virtual whiteboards, to create a shared workspace and repository for project information, roles, and responsibilities.
- Providing training and resources on effective collaboration, communication, and coordination skills, and modeling these behaviors in their own leadership and interactions with the team.
- Encouraging team members to take ownership and initiative in their roles and responsibilities, and to propose and implement their own ideas for improving collaboration and coordination within the team.
- Continuously seeking feedback and input from team members and stakeholders on the effectiveness and clarity of the team's roles and responsibilities, and using this information to identify areas for improvement and to adjust strategies and tactics accordingly.

By defining clear roles and responsibilities and promoting effective team collaboration in a remote project setting, project managers can create a team environment that is efficient, productive, and enjoyable for all team members. When team members have a clear understanding of their roles and expectations, and feel empowered and supported to collaborate and contribute their best work, they are more likely to be engaged, motivated, and successful in achieving the project goals and delivering high-quality results.

So if you're a remote project manager, make defining clear roles and responsibilities and promoting effective team collaboration a top priority. Clarify project goals, deliverables, and timeline, define roles and responsibilities using a RACI matrix, align roles and responsibilities with skills, strengths, and interests, foster a culture of collaboration and shared ownership, establish clear communication and coordination protocols, and continuously monitor and adjust roles and responsibilities. By investing in your team's collaboration and coordination skills and practices, you'll be well-equipped to build a remote team that is efficient, effective, and successful.

Setting Team Goals and Expectations

In a remote project setting, setting clear and measurable team goals and expectations is crucial for aligning team members' efforts, motivating their performance, and ensuring successful project outcomes. When team members have a shared understanding of what they are working towards, what is expected of them, and how their individual contributions fit into the bigger picture, they are more likely to be engaged, focused, and accountable for their work. As a remote project manager, it's your responsibility to define and communicate team goals and expectations, and to create a framework for monitoring and measuring progress and success.

Here are some key strategies for setting team goals and expectations in a remote project setting:

1. Align team goals with project and organizational objectives
- Ensure that the team goals are directly aligned with and support the overall project goals, deliverables, and timeline, as well as the broader organizational strategy and priorities.
- Communicate the connection between the team goals and the project and organizational objectives clearly and consistently, so that team members understand the bigger picture and the value of their contributions.
- Seek input and buy-in from team members and stakeholders on the team goals, to ensure that they are realistic, relevant, and meaningful to everyone involved.

2. Make team goals specific, measurable, achievable, relevant, and time-bound (SMART)
- Use the SMART framework to define team goals that are specific (clearly defined and unambiguous), measurable (quantifiable and trackable), achievable (realistic and attainable), relevant (aligned with project and organizational objectives), and time-bound (with clear deadlines and milestones).
- Break down larger team goals into smaller, actionable sub-goals or objectives, and assign clear owners and due dates for each one, using a project management tool or template.
- Communicate the SMART team goals clearly and consistently to all team members, and ensure that everyone understands the criteria for success and how progress will be measured and reported.

3. Define expectations for team member performance and behavior
- In addition to setting team goals, define clear expectations for individual team member performance and behavior, such as quality standards, communication protocols, collaboration practices, and work ethics.
- Use a team charter, job descriptions, or performance agreements to document and communicate these expectations, and ensure that all team members have access to and understand these documents.
- Provide examples and models of desired performance and behavior, and reinforce these expectations through regular feedback, coaching, and recognition.

4. Establish a system for monitoring and measuring progress and success
- Implement a system for regularly monitoring and measuring progress and success towards the team goals and expectations, using metrics, milestones, and deliverables as key indicators.
- Use project management tools, dashboards, or reports to track and visualize progress and performance data, and share this information transparently and consistently with the team and stakeholders.
- Establish a cadence of regular check-ins, reviews, or retrospectives to discuss progress, challenges, and learnings, and to make any necessary adjustments or course corrections.

5. Provide support and resources for achieving team goals and expectations
- Ensure that team members have access to the necessary tools, information, and resources to achieve the team goals and meet the expectations, such as technology, training, or subject matter expertise.
- Provide ongoing support, guidance, and coaching to help team members overcome obstacles, develop new skills, and maintain motivation and focus towards the goals.
- Foster a culture of psychological safety, where team members feel comfortable asking for help, admitting mistakes, and learning from failures, without fear of judgment or retribution.

6. Celebrate and recognize progress and achievements
- Regularly celebrate and recognize team and individual progress and achievements towards the goals and expectations, using a variety of formal and informal methods, such as shout-outs, awards, or bonuses.
- Communicate the impact and value of the team's work to the project, organization, and stakeholders, and showcase how their efforts are making a difference and contributing to success.
- Encourage team members to celebrate and recognize each other's successes and contributions, and create a culture of appreciation, gratitude, and mutual support.

Setting team goals and expectations in a remote project setting requires intentional and collaborative effort from project managers and team members alike. It involves aligning team goals with project and organizational objectives, making goals SMART and actionable, defining expectations for performance and behavior, establishing a system for monitoring and measuring progress and success, providing support and resources for achieving goals and expectations, and celebrating and recognizing progress and achievements.

To overcome the challenges of setting team goals and expectations in a remote setting, project managers can use a variety of strategies, such as:
- Using virtual collaboration tools and platforms, such as video conferencing, online whiteboards, or project management software, to facilitate interactive and engaging goal-setting and expectation-setting sessions with the team.

- Providing training and resources on effective goal-setting, performance management, and feedback techniques, and modeling these practices in their own leadership and interactions with the team.
- Encouraging team members to take ownership and accountability for their individual goals and expectations, and to propose and implement their own strategies for achieving and exceeding them.
- Continuously seeking feedback and input from team members and stakeholders on the relevance, clarity, and achievability of the team goals and expectations, and using this information to identify areas for improvement and to adjust strategies and tactics accordingly.

By setting clear and measurable team goals and expectations in a remote project setting, project managers can create a team environment that is focused, motivated, and accountable for delivering high-quality results and achieving project success. When team members have a shared understanding of what they are working towards, what is expected of them, and how their efforts contribute to the bigger picture, they are more likely to be engaged, committed, and high-performing in their work.

So if you're a remote project manager, make setting team goals and expectations a top priority. Align team goals with project and organizational objectives, make goals SMART and actionable, define expectations for performance and behavior, establish a system for monitoring and measuring progress and success, provide support and resources for achieving goals and expectations, and celebrate and recognize progress and achievements.

By investing in your team's goal-setting and expectation-setting practices, you'll be well-equipped to build a remote team that is focused, motivated, and successful.

Facilitating Brainstorming and Problem-Solving Sessions

In a remote project setting, facilitating effective brainstorming and problem-solving sessions is essential for fostering creativity, innovation, and collaboration among team members. When team members are able to generate and share new ideas, challenge assumptions, and work together to solve complex problems, they are more likely to deliver high-quality results, overcome obstacles, and achieve project success. As a remote project manager, it's your responsibility to create a framework and environment for effective brainstorming and problem-solving, and to facilitate these sessions in a way that maximizes participation, engagement, and outcomes.

Here are some key strategies for facilitating brainstorming and problem-solving sessions in a remote project setting:

1. Define the purpose, scope, and desired outcomes of the session

- Clearly define the purpose, scope, and desired outcomes of the brainstorming or problem-solving session, and communicate these to the team in advance, along with any relevant background information or context.
- Ensure that the session is focused on a specific problem, challenge, or opportunity that is relevant and meaningful to the project and the team, and that the desired outcomes are realistic and achievable within the available time and resources.

- Seek input and buy-in from team members and stakeholders on the purpose, scope, and desired outcomes of the session, to ensure that everyone is aligned and committed to the process and the results.

2. Choose the right tools and techniques for remote facilitation
- Select the appropriate tools and techniques for facilitating the brainstorming or problem-solving session remotely, based on the size and composition of the team, the nature of the problem or challenge, and the desired outcomes.
- Use virtual collaboration tools and platforms, such as video conferencing, online whiteboards, or mind mapping software, to create an interactive and engaging environment for ideation and discussion.
- Consider using structured brainstorming or problem-solving techniques, such as brainwriting, nominal group technique, or design thinking, to guide and stimulate the team's thinking and creativity.

3. Set the stage for psychological safety and inclusivity
- Create a psychologically safe and inclusive environment for the brainstorming or problem-solving session, where all team members feel comfortable sharing their ideas, opinions, and perspectives, without fear of judgment, criticism, or retribution.
- Establish clear ground rules and expectations for participation, such as active listening, respectful communication, and constructive feedback, and model these behaviors in your own facilitation and interactions with the team.

- Encourage and celebrate diversity of thought and perspective, and actively seek out and value contributions from all team members, regardless of their role, experience, or background.

4. Facilitate ideation and discussion using effective questioning and probing
- Use effective questioning and probing techniques to stimulate and guide the team's ideation and discussion, such as open-ended questions, clarifying questions, or provocative statements.
- Encourage team members to build on each other's ideas, challenge assumptions, and explore alternative perspectives and solutions, using techniques such as "yes, and" or "what if" statements.
- Capture and document all ideas and contributions using a shared virtual whiteboard or document, and ensure that everyone has access to and can contribute to this artifact throughout the session.

5. Synthesize and prioritize ideas and solutions using structured decision-making
- Once the team has generated a range of ideas and potential solutions, use structured decision-making techniques to synthesize, evaluate, and prioritize these options, based on criteria such as feasibility, impact, and alignment with project goals and constraints.
- Use tools such as decision matrices, dot voting, or weighted scoring to facilitate the team's decision-making process, and ensure that everyone has an equal voice and vote in the outcome.

- Document the final decisions and action items from the session, and ensure that everyone understands and commits to the next steps and responsibilities for implementation and follow-up.

6. Debrief and reflect on the session to identify learnings and improvements
    - After the brainstorming or problem-solving session, conduct a debrief and reflection with the team to identify what worked well, what could be improved, and what insights or learnings emerged from the process.
    - Seek feedback and input from team members on their experience and satisfaction with the session, using techniques such as plus/delta or retrospective templates.
    - Use the insights and learnings from the debrief to refine and improve the team's brainstorming and problem-solving practices, and to identify opportunities for further collaboration and innovation in the project.

Facilitating effective brainstorming and problem-solving sessions in a remote project setting requires intentional and skillful effort from project managers and team members alike. It involves defining the purpose, scope, and desired outcomes of the session, choosing the right tools and techniques for remote facilitation, setting the stage for psychological safety and inclusivity, facilitating ideation and discussion using effective questioning and probing, synthesizing and prioritizing ideas and solutions using structured decision-making, and debriefing and reflecting on the session to identify learnings and improvements.

To overcome the challenges of facilitating brainstorming and problem-solving sessions in a remote setting, project managers can use a variety of strategies, such as:

- Providing training and resources on effective facilitation, communication, and collaboration skills, and modeling these practices in their own leadership and interactions with the team.
- Encouraging team members to take ownership and leadership in the brainstorming and problem-solving process, and to propose and implement their own ideas and solutions for the project.
- Continuously seeking feedback and input from team members and stakeholders on the effectiveness and value of the brainstorming and problem-solving sessions, and using this information to identify areas for improvement and to adjust strategies and tactics accordingly.
- Celebrating and recognizing the team's creativity, innovation, and problem-solving successes, and communicating the impact and value of their contributions to the project and the organization.

By facilitating effective brainstorming and problem-solving sessions in a remote project setting, project managers can create a team environment that is creative, collaborative, and resilient in the face of challenges and uncertainties. When team members are able to generate and share new ideas, challenge assumptions, and work together to solve complex problems, they are more likely to be engaged, motivated, and high-performing in their work, and to deliver outstanding results for the project and the organization.

So if you're a remote project manager, make facilitating brainstorming and problem-solving sessions a top priority. Define the purpose, scope, and desired outcomes of the session, choose the right tools and techniques for remote facilitation, set the stage for psychological safety and inclusivity, facilitate ideation and discussion using effective questioning and probing, synthesize and prioritize ideas and solutions using structured decision-making, and debrief and reflect on the session to identify learnings and improvements. By investing in your team's brainstorming and problem-solving skills and practices, you'll be well-equipped to build a remote team that is creative, collaborative, and successful.

Encouraging Knowledge Sharing and Peer Support

In a remote project setting, encouraging knowledge sharing and peer support is crucial for fostering a culture of continuous learning, collaboration, and mutual support among team members. When team members are able to share their expertise, insights, and experiences with each other, and to seek and provide help and guidance when needed, they are more likely to grow and develop in their roles, overcome challenges and obstacles, and contribute to the overall success of the project. As a remote project manager, it's your responsibility to create a framework and environment for effective knowledge sharing and peer support, and to facilitate and encourage these practices among your team.

Here are some key strategies for encouraging knowledge sharing and peer support in a remote project setting:

1. Establish a culture of openness, trust, and psychological safety
- Create a team culture that values and promotes openness, trust, and psychological safety, where team members feel comfortable sharing their knowledge, asking for help, and admitting mistakes or uncertainties, without fear of judgment, criticism, or retribution.
- Model and reinforce these values through your own leadership and communication style, by being transparent, authentic, and vulnerable in your interactions with the team, and by actively seeking and valuing their input and feedback.

- Establish clear norms and expectations for knowledge sharing and peer support, such as active listening, constructive feedback, and respectful communication, and hold team members accountable for upholding these standards.

2. Provide multiple channels and platforms for knowledge sharing and peer support

- Offer a variety of channels and platforms for team members to share knowledge and seek peer support, such as virtual communities of practice, discussion forums, wikis, or mentoring programs, based on their preferences and needs.
- Use synchronous and asynchronous communication tools, such as video conferencing, instant messaging, or email, to facilitate real-time and ongoing knowledge sharing and peer support among team members, regardless of their location or time zone.
- Ensure that these channels and platforms are easily accessible, user-friendly, and integrated with the team's existing workflows and tools, to minimize barriers to participation and engagement.

3. Encourage and facilitate regular knowledge sharing and peer support activities

- Schedule and facilitate regular knowledge sharing and peer support activities, such as brown bag lunches, lightning talks, or peer review sessions, to create dedicated time and space for team members to share their expertise and learn from each other.

- Use structured formats and agendas for these activities, such as presentations, demos, or case studies, to ensure that the content is relevant, engaging, and actionable for the team, and that everyone has an opportunity to contribute and participate.
- Encourage team members to take ownership and leadership of these activities, by proposing topics, facilitating sessions, or sharing their own experiences and insights, and provide them with the necessary support and resources to do so effectively.

4. Recognize and reward knowledge sharing and peer support behaviors

- Recognize and reward team members who demonstrate exceptional knowledge sharing and peer support behaviors, such as proactively sharing their expertise, helping others overcome challenges, or mentoring new team members, using a variety of formal and informal methods, such as public acknowledgments, bonuses, or development opportunities.
- Communicate the value and impact of these behaviors to the team and the organization, by highlighting how they contribute to the project's success, the team's growth and development, and the company's culture and values.
- Encourage team members to recognize and appreciate each other's knowledge sharing and peer support efforts, by providing feedback, thanks, or kudos, and by nominating each other for awards or recognition programs.

5. Provide resources and support for continuous learning and development

- Invest in the team's continuous learning and development, by providing access to relevant training, courses, conferences, or other educational resources, based on their skills, interests, and career goals.
- Encourage team members to share their learning experiences and insights with each other, by presenting key takeaways, leading discussions, or applying new knowledge to the project, and provide them with the necessary time and support to do so.
- Foster a growth mindset and a culture of experimentation and innovation, by encouraging team members to take risks, try new approaches, and learn from failures, and by providing them with a safe and supportive environment to do so.

6. Measure and evaluate the impact and effectiveness of knowledge sharing and peer support

- Establish metrics and indicators to measure and evaluate the impact and effectiveness of the team's knowledge sharing and peer support practices, such as participation rates, satisfaction scores, or performance improvements, and use this data to identify areas for improvement and optimization.
- Seek regular feedback and input from team members and stakeholders on the value and relevance of these practices, using surveys, interviews, or focus groups, and use this information to refine and adapt the team's approach and strategies.

- Celebrate and communicate the successes and achievements of the team's knowledge sharing and peer support efforts, by sharing case studies, testimonials, or impact stories, and by showcasing how these practices contribute to the project's and the organization's goals and values.

Encouraging knowledge sharing and peer support in a remote project setting requires intentional and sustained effort from project managers and team members alike. It involves establishing a culture of openness, trust, and psychological safety, providing multiple channels and platforms for knowledge sharing and peer support, encouraging and facilitating regular knowledge sharing and peer support activities, recognizing and rewarding knowledge sharing and peer support behaviors, providing resources and support for continuous learning and development, and measuring and evaluating the impact and effectiveness of knowledge sharing and peer support.

To overcome the challenges of encouraging knowledge sharing and peer support in a remote setting, project managers can use a variety of strategies, such as:

- Using virtual collaboration tools and platforms, such as knowledge management systems, social learning platforms, or peer coaching software, to facilitate and streamline knowledge sharing and peer support among team members.

- Providing training and resources on effective knowledge sharing, communication, and collaboration skills, and modeling these practices in their own leadership and interactions with the team.
- Encouraging team members to take ownership and accountability for their own learning and development, and to seek out and engage in knowledge sharing and peer support opportunities that align with their goals and interests.
- Continuously seeking feedback and input from team members and stakeholders on the effectiveness and value of the team's knowledge sharing and peer support practices, and using this information to identify areas for improvement and to adjust strategies and tactics accordingly.

By encouraging knowledge sharing and peer support in a remote project setting, project managers can create a team environment that is collaborative, supportive, and growth-oriented, where team members are able to learn from each other, overcome challenges together, and achieve their full potential in their roles and careers. When team members are empowered and motivated to share their knowledge and expertise, and to seek and provide help and guidance when needed, they are more likely to be engaged, committed, and high-performing in their work, and to contribute to the overall success and impact of the project and the organization.

So if you're a remote project manager, make encouraging knowledge sharing and peer support a top priority. Establish a culture of openness, trust, and psychological safety, provide multiple channels and platforms for knowledge sharing and peer support, encourage and facilitate regular knowledge sharing and peer support activities, recognize and reward knowledge sharing and peer support behaviors, provide resources and support for continuous learning and development, and measure and evaluate the impact and effectiveness of knowledge sharing and peer support. By investing in your team's knowledge sharing and peer support practices, you'll be well-equipped to build a remote team that is collaborative, supportive, and successful.

Chapter 9
Managing Team Performance and Development
Setting Performance Metrics and KPIs

In a remote project setting, managing team performance and development is essential for ensuring that team members are meeting their goals, delivering high-quality work, and growing in their roles and careers. When team members have clear performance expectations, regular feedback and coaching, and opportunities for learning and development, they are more likely to be engaged, motivated, and successful in their work, and to contribute to the overall success of the project and the organization. As a remote project manager, it's your responsibility to establish a framework and process for managing team performance and development, and to provide ongoing support and guidance to help team members achieve their full potential.

One key aspect of managing team performance and development is setting performance metrics and key performance indicators (KPIs). These are quantifiable measures that track and evaluate team members' progress and success in meeting their goals and expectations, and that provide a basis for feedback, recognition, and improvement. Here are some key strategies for setting performance metrics and KPIs in a remote project setting:

1. Align performance metrics and KPIs with project and organizational goals
- Ensure that the performance metrics and KPIs for each team member are directly aligned with and support the overall goals and objectives of the project and the organization, and that they are relevant and meaningful to the team member's role and responsibilities.
- Communicate the connection between individual performance and project and organizational success clearly and consistently, so that team members understand the bigger picture and the value of their contributions.
- Seek input and buy-in from team members and stakeholders on the performance metrics and KPIs, to ensure that they are realistic, achievable, and motivating for everyone involved.

2. Make performance metrics and KPIs specific, measurable, achievable, relevant, and time-bound (SMART)
- Use the SMART framework to define performance metrics and KPIs that are specific (clearly defined and unambiguous), measurable (quantifiable and trackable), achievable (realistic and attainable), relevant (aligned with project organizational goals), and time-bound (with clear deadlines and milestones).
- Break down larger performance goals into smaller, actionable objectives or key results, and assign clear owners and due dates for each one, using a performance management tool or template.

- Communicate the SMART performance metrics and KPIs clearly and consistently to each team member, and ensure that they understand the criteria for success and how progress will be measured and reported.

3. Use a variety of performance metrics and KPIs to capture different aspects of performance

- Include a mix of quantitative and qualitative performance metrics and KPIs, such as output metrics (e.g., number of tasks completed, lines of code written), quality metrics (e.g., error rates, customer satisfaction scores), and process metrics (e.g., adherence to standards, collaboration and communication effectiveness).
- Use a balanced scorecard approach to capture different perspectives on performance, such as financial, customer, internal process, and learning and growth, and to ensure that the metrics and KPIs are comprehensive and holistic.
- Tailor the performance metrics and KPIs to each team member's role, level, and development goals, and ensure that they are challenging but achievable, and that they provide opportunities for growth and recognition.

4. Establish a regular cadence for tracking and reviewing performance metrics and KPIs

- Set up a regular schedule for tracking and reviewing each team member's performance metrics and KPIs, such as weekly check-ins, monthly reviews, or quarterly evaluations, and ensure that both the manager and the team member are prepared and engaged in these conversations.

- Use a consistent format and agenda for these performance conversations, such as the SBI (situation, behavior, impact) feedback model, the GROW (goal, reality, options, way forward) coaching framework, or the 5 Conversations (goal setting, praising, redirecting, wrapping up, following up) approach, to ensure that the discussions are productive, actionable, and motivating.
- Document the key takeaways, action items, and next steps from each performance conversation, and ensure that both the manager and the team member have access to and are accountable for following through on these commitments.

5. Use performance metrics and KPIs to provide ongoing feedback, coaching, and development
- Use the performance metrics and KPIs as a basis for providing regular, timely, and specific feedback and coaching to each team member, both on their strengths and areas for improvement, and on how they can continue to grow and develop in their role and career.
- Provide a mix of positive and constructive feedback, using a ratio of at least 3:1, and ensure that the feedback is based on observable behaviors and outcomes, rather than on personality or assumptions.
- Use the performance metrics and KPIs to identify development opportunities and goals for each team member, such as training, mentoring, or stretch assignments, and work with them to create a personalized development plan that aligns with their interests, skills, and aspirations.

6. Celebrate and recognize performance achievements and successes

- Use the performance metrics and KPIs to identify and celebrate individual and team achievements and successes, such as exceeding targets, delivering high-quality work, or demonstrating exceptional collaboration or innovation, and ensure that the recognition is timely, specific, and meaningful.
- Use a variety of recognition methods and channels, such as public acknowledgments, bonuses, or development opportunities, to show appreciation and reinforce the desired behaviors and outcomes, and to create a culture of high performance and continuous improvement.
- Encourage team members to recognize and appreciate each other's performance and contributions, by providing peer feedback, kudos, or nominations, and by celebrating team successes and milestones together.

Setting performance metrics and KPIs is a critical foundation for managing team performance and development in a remote project setting. It provides a clear, measurable, and actionable framework for setting expectations, tracking progress, providing feedback and coaching, and recognizing and rewarding success. However, it's important to remember that performance metrics and KPIs are not an end in themselves, but rather a means to support and enhance team members' growth, engagement, and impact.

To overcome the challenges of setting performance metrics and KPIs in a remote setting, project managers can use a variety of strategies, such as:

- Using virtual performance management tools and platforms, such as goal-setting software, feedback and coaching apps, or learning management systems, to facilitate and streamline the performance management process and conversations.
- Providing training and resources on effective performance management, feedback, and coaching skills, and modeling these practices in their own leadership and interactions with the team.
- Encouraging team members to take ownership and accountability for their own performance and development, and to seek out and engage in feedback and coaching conversations that align with their goals and interests.
- Continuously seeking feedback and input from team members and stakeholders on the effectiveness and value of the performance metrics and KPIs, and using this information to identify areas for improvement and to adjust strategies and tactics accordingly.

By setting clear, measurable, and actionable performance metrics and KPIs, and using them to provide ongoing feedback, coaching, and development, project managers can create a team environment that is high-performing, growth-oriented, and impactful, where team members are able to achieve their full potential and contribute to the success of the project and the organization.

So if you're a remote project manager, make setting performance metrics and KPIs a top priority. Align performance metrics and KPIs with project and organizational goals, make them SMART and balanced, use a variety of metrics and KPIs to capture different aspects of performance, establish a regular cadence for tracking and reviewing performance, use performance metrics and KPIs to provide ongoing feedback, coaching, and development, and celebrate and recognize performance achievements and successes. By investing in your team's performance management and development practices, you'll be well-equipped to build a remote team that is high-performing, engaged, and successful.

Providing Regular Feedback and Coaching

In a remote project setting, providing regular feedback and coaching is crucial for supporting team members' performance, growth, and development. When team members receive timely, specific, and actionable feedback on their work and behavior, and when they have access to ongoing coaching and guidance from their manager and peers, they are more likely to feel valued, engaged, and motivated in their roles, and to continuously improve and excel in their performance. As a remote project manager, it's your responsibility to create a culture and process for providing regular feedback and coaching to your team members, and to equip yourself and your team with the skills and tools to do so effectively.

Here are some key strategies for providing regular feedback and coaching in a remote project setting:

1. Establish a regular cadence and format for feedback and coaching conversations
- Set up a consistent schedule and format for providing feedback and coaching to each team member, such as weekly one-on-one meetings, monthly performance check-ins, or quarterly development reviews, and ensure that both the manager and the team member are prepared and engaged in these conversations.
- Use a structured approach and agenda for these conversations, such as the SBI (situation, behavior, impact) feedback model, the GROW (goal, reality,

- options, way forward) coaching framework, or the 5 Conversations (goal setting, praising, redirecting, wrapping up, following up) approach, to ensure that the discussions are focused, productive, and action-oriented.
- Ensure that the feedback and coaching conversations are two-way dialogues, where both the manager and the team member have opportunities to share their perspectives, ask questions, and provide input and suggestions, and where the focus is on problem-solving and continuous improvement, rather than on judgment or blame.

2. Provide timely, specific, and actionable feedback based on observable behaviors and outcomes
- Provide feedback to team members as soon as possible after observing a specific behavior or outcome, ideally within 24-48 hours, to ensure that the feedback is relevant, meaningful, and easy to remember and act upon.
- Use specific and observable examples and data to illustrate the behavior or outcome that you are providing feedback on, rather than relying on general statements or assumptions, and ensure that the feedback is focused on the behavior or outcome itself, rather than on the person's character or intentions.
- Provide actionable suggestions and guidance on how the team member can improve or build upon the behavior or outcome, and work with them to identify specific next steps and resources that they can use to implement the feedback and achieve their goals.

3. Use a mix of positive and constructive feedback to reinforce strengths and address areas for improvement
- Provide a balanced mix of positive and constructive feedback to team members, using a ratio of at least 3:1, to ensure that the feedback is motivating, encouraging, and focused on growth and development, rather than on criticism or punishment.
- Use positive feedback to recognize and reinforce the team member's strengths, accomplishments, and contributions, and to show appreciation and encouragement for their efforts and progress, using specific examples and impact statements to illustrate the value and significance of their work.
- Use constructive feedback to address areas for improvement or development, using a neutral and non-judgmental tone, and focusing on the specific behaviors or outcomes that need to change or improve, rather than on the person's character or abilities, and providing clear and actionable guidance on how to do so.

4. Provide ongoing coaching and guidance to support team members' development and growth
- In addition to providing feedback on specific behaviors and outcomes, provide ongoing coaching and guidance to team members to support their overall development and growth in their roles and careers, using a collaborative and empowering approach that builds on their strengths and interests.

- Use coaching techniques such as active listening, powerful questioning, and reflective feedback to help team members clarify their goals, identify their challenges and opportunities, generate creative solutions and strategies, and take ownership and accountability for their own development and success.
- Provide resources and support for team members' learning and development, such as training, mentoring, or stretch assignments, and work with them to create personalized development plans that align with their aspirations and the needs of the project and the organization.

5. Foster a culture of continuous feedback and coaching among team members

- Encourage and equip team members to provide feedback and coaching to each other, in addition to receiving it from their manager, to create a culture of continuous learning, collaboration, and peer support, and to build a shared sense of accountability and ownership for the team's performance and success.
- Provide training and resources on effective feedback and coaching skills, such as active listening, assertive communication, and empathy, and model these skills in your own interactions and leadership style, to create a safe and supportive environment for giving and receiving feedback and coaching.

- Celebrate and recognize team members who demonstrate a commitment to continuous feedback and coaching, by providing peer feedback and recognition, sharing best practices and success stories, and creating opportunities for team members to lead and facilitate feedback and coaching conversations and initiatives.

6. Use feedback and coaching to inform performance evaluations and development plans

- Use the feedback and coaching conversations as a basis for conducting formal performance evaluations and creating development plans for each team member, ensuring that the evaluations and plans are fair, accurate, and aligned with the team member's goals and performance metrics.
- Provide clear and specific examples and data from the feedback and coaching conversations to support the performance ratings and development recommendations, and ensure that the team member has opportunities to provide input and feedback on the evaluation and plan, and to discuss any concerns or disagreements.
- Use the performance evaluations and development plans as a tool for ongoing performance management and development, by setting clear expectations and goals, tracking progress and accomplishments, providing regular feedback and coaching, and recognizing and rewarding success and improvement.

Providing regular feedback and coaching is a critical skill and practice for managing team performance and development in a remote project setting. It enables project managers to support and guide team members' growth and success, to address performance issues and challenges proactively and constructively, and to create a culture of continuous learning, collaboration, and excellence. However, it's important to remember that feedback and coaching are not one-size-fits-all, and that different team members may have different preferences, styles, and needs when it comes to receiving and acting on feedback and coaching.

To overcome the challenges of providing regular feedback and coaching in a remote setting, project managers can use a variety of strategies, such as:

- Using virtual communication and collaboration tools, such as video conferencing, instant messaging, or feedback and coaching apps, to facilitate regular, timely, and engaging feedback and coaching conversations, regardless of location or time zone.
- Providing training and resources on effective feedback and coaching techniques, such as the SBI model, the GROW framework, or the 5 Conversations approach, and practicing and refining these skills through role-playing, case studies, or peer feedback.
- Encouraging team members to take ownership and initiative in seeking and providing feedback and coaching, by setting up peer feedback and coaching systems, sharing feedback and coaching success stories and best practices, and recognizing and rewarding feedback and coaching champions and role models.

- Continuously seeking feedback and input from team members and stakeholders on the effectiveness and value of the feedback and coaching practices, and using this information to identify areas for improvement and to adjust strategies and tactics accordingly.

By providing regular, specific, and actionable feedback and coaching, and by fostering a culture of continuous learning and development, project managers can create a team environment that is high-performing, growth-oriented, and impactful, where team members are able to achieve their full potential and contribute to the success of the project and the organization.

So if you're a remote project manager, make providing regular feedback and coaching a top priority. Establish a regular cadence and format for feedback and coaching conversations, provide timely, specific, and actionable feedback based on observable behaviors and outcomes, use a mix of positive and constructive feedback to reinforce strengths and address areas for improvement, provide ongoing coaching and guidance to support team members' development and growth, foster a culture of continuous feedback and coaching among team members, and use feedback and coaching to inform performance evaluations and development plans. By investing in your own and your team's feedback and coaching skills and practices, you'll be well-equipped to build a remote team that is high-performing, engaged, and successful.

Conducting Virtual Performance Reviews

In a remote project setting, conducting virtual performance reviews is an essential part of managing team performance and development. Performance reviews provide an opportunity for project managers and team members to reflect on their accomplishments, challenges, and growth opportunities, to set goals and expectations for the future, and to discuss any issues or concerns that may be impacting their work or well-being. When conducted effectively, virtual performance reviews can help to build trust, accountability, and engagement among team members, and to align their individual performance and development with the goals and needs of the project and the organization. As a remote project manager, it's your responsibility to design and facilitate a virtual performance review process that is fair, meaningful, and productive for your team members.

Here are some key strategies for conducting virtual performance reviews in a remote project setting:

1. **Prepare for the performance review in advance**
   - Schedule the performance review meeting well in advance, ideally at least 2-4 weeks ahead of time, to ensure that both the manager and the team member have sufficient time to prepare and gather relevant information and feedback.
   - Provide clear guidelines and expectations for the performance review process, including the purpose, format, and agenda of the meeting, the performance

- metrics and criteria that will be used to evaluate the team member's performance, and any pre-work or documentation that the team member needs to complete or submit prior to the meeting.
- Gather and review relevant data and feedback on the team member's performance, including their job description, performance goals and metrics, feedback and coaching notes, and any other relevant documentation or input from stakeholders or peers, to ensure that the performance review is based on a comprehensive and objective assessment of their work and contributions.

2. Create a safe and supportive environment for the performance review conversation
- Set a positive and collaborative tone for the performance review conversation, by expressing appreciation for the team member's contributions and efforts, and by emphasizing the purpose of the meeting as a two-way dialogue focused on growth, development, and continuous improvement.
- Use video conferencing and other virtual communication tools to create a sense of presence and connection during the performance review conversation, and to pick up on nonverbal cues and emotions that may be harder to detect through audio or written communication alone.
- Ensure that the performance review conversation is conducted in a private and confidential setting, free from distractions or interruptions, and that both the manager and the team member have a stable and reliable internet connection and a quiet and comfortable workspace.

3. Use a structured and balanced approach to discussing performance and development
- Use a structured and consistent format and agenda for the performance review conversation, such as the SBI (situation, behavior, impact) feedback model, the GROW (goal, reality, options, way forward) coaching framework, or the 5 Conversations (goal setting, praising, redirecting, wrapping up, following up) approach, to ensure that the discussion is focused, productive, and action-oriented.
- Provide a balanced and comprehensive assessment of the team member's performance, by discussing both their strengths and accomplishments, as well as any areas for improvement or development, using specific examples and data to support your observations and feedback.
- Use open-ended questions and active listening techniques to encourage the team member to share their own perspectives, insights, and ideas on their performance and development, and to identify any challenges, obstacles, or support needs that they may have.

4. Set clear and measurable goals and expectations for the future
- Based on the performance review discussion, work with the team member to set clear, specific, and measurable goals and expectations for their performance and development in the upcoming period, aligned with the project and organizational goals and priorities.

- Use the SMART (specific, measurable, achievable, relevant, time-bound) framework to ensure that the goals and expectations are realistic, challenging, and motivating for the team member, and that they have a clear understanding of what success looks like and how it will be measured and evaluated.
- Identify any resources, support, or development opportunities that the team member may need to achieve their goals and expectations, such as training, mentoring, or stretch assignments, and work with them to create a plan and timeline for accessing and utilizing these resources.

5. Follow up and follow through on the performance review outcomes and commitments

- Document the key outcomes, goals, and commitments from the performance review conversation in a clear and concise performance review summary or development plan, and share it with the team member and any other relevant stakeholders, such as HR or senior leadership.
- Schedule regular check-ins and follow-up conversations with the team member to review their progress and performance against their goals and expectations, to provide ongoing feedback and coaching, and to make any necessary adjustments or course corrections based on changing circumstances or needs.
- Celebrate and recognize the team member's successes and achievements in meeting their goals and expectations, using a variety of recognition and reward methods, such as public acknowledgment, bonuses, or development opportunities, and encourage them to continue to grow and excel in their role and career.

- Use the SMART (specific, measurable, achievable, relevant, time-bound) framework to ensure that the goals and expectations are realistic, challenging, and motivating for the team member, and that they have a clear understanding of what success looks like and how it will be measured and evaluated.
- Identify any resources, support, or development opportunities that the team member may need to achieve their goals and expectations, such as training, mentoring, or stretch assignments, and work with them to create a plan and timeline for accessing and utilizing these resources.

5. Follow up and follow through on the performance review outcomes and commitments
- Document the key outcomes, goals, and commitments from the performance review conversation in a clear and concise performance review summary or development plan, and share it with the team member and any other relevant stakeholders, such as HR or senior leadership.
- Schedule regular check-ins and follow-up conversations with the team member to review their progress and performance against their goals and expectations, to provide ongoing feedback and coaching, and to make any necessary adjustments or course corrections based on changing circumstances or needs.
- Celebrate and recognize the team member's successes and achievements in meeting their goals and expectations, using a variety of recognition and reward methods, such as public acknowledgment, bonuses, or development opportunities, and encourage them to continue to grow and excel in their role and career.

6. **Continuously improve and adapt the virtual performance review process based on feedback and lessons learned**
    - Seek feedback and input from team members and stakeholders on their experience and satisfaction with the virtual performance review process, using surveys, focus groups, or individual conversations, and use this feedback to identify areas for improvement and innovation in the process and tools.
    - Continuously monitor and evaluate the effectiveness and impact of the virtual performance review process on team member performance, engagement, and development, using metrics such as goal achievement, retention, and promotion rates, and use this data to make data-driven decisions and adjustments to the process and approach.
    - Stay up-to-date on best practices and trends in virtual performance management and development, by attending webinars, reading articles and case studies, and connecting with other remote project managers and HR professionals, and incorporate relevant insights and ideas into your own virtual performance review process and practices.

Conducting virtual performance reviews can be challenging, especially in a remote project setting where team members may be working across different time zones, cultures, and communication styles. However, by following these strategies and best practices, project managers can create a virtual performance review process that is fair, meaningful, and productive for their team members, and that supports their ongoing performance, growth, and success in their roles and careers.

To overcome the challenges of conducting virtual performance reviews in a remote setting, project managers can use a variety of strategies, such as:

- Using performance management software and tools, such as goal-setting and tracking apps, 360-degree feedback platforms, or performance review templates and checklists, to streamline and standardize the virtual performance review process and documentation.
- Providing training and resources on effective virtual communication and collaboration skills, such as active listening, empathy, and assertiveness, and modeling these skills in their own interactions and leadership style, to create a safe and supportive environment for virtual performance review conversations.
- Encouraging team members to take ownership and accountability for their own performance and development, by setting their own goals and expectations, seeking feedback and coaching from their manager and peers, and tracking and reporting on their own progress and accomplishments.
- Continuously seeking feedback and input from team members and stakeholders on the effectiveness and value of the virtual performance review process, and using this information to identify areas for improvement and to adjust strategies and tactics accordingly.

By conducting virtual performance reviews that are structured, balanced, and action-oriented, and by continuously improving and adapting the process based on feedback and lessons learned, project managers can create a team environment that is high-performing, growth-oriented, and impactful, where team members are able to achieve their full potential and contribute to the success of the project and the organization.

So if you're a remote project manager, make conducting virtual performance reviews a top priority. Prepare for the performance review in advance, create a safe and supportive environment for the performance review conversation, use a structured and balanced approach to discussing performance and development, set clear and measurable goals and expectations for the future, follow up and follow through on the performance review outcomes and commitments, and continuously improve and adapt the virtual performance review process based on feedback and lessons learned. By investing in your own and your team's virtual performance review skills and practices, you'll be well-equipped to build a remote team that is high-performing, engaged, and successful.

Supporting Professional Development and Growth

In a remote project setting, supporting team members' professional development and growth is a critical responsibility of project managers. When team members have opportunities to learn new skills, take on new challenges, and advance their careers, they are more likely to be engaged, motivated, and committed to their work and to the organization. Moreover, investing in team members' professional development and growth can help to build a strong talent pipeline, enhance the team's collective capabilities and performance, and create a culture of continuous learning and innovation. As a remote project manager, it's your role to create an environment and provide resources and support that enable your team members to grow and thrive in their roles and careers.

Here are some key strategies for supporting professional development and growth in a remote project setting:

1. Assess team members' skills, interests, and aspirations
- Conduct regular skills assessments and career development conversations with each team member, to understand their current capabilities, areas for improvement, and long-term career goals and aspirations.
- Use tools such as skills matrices, career path frameworks, or individual development plans to map out each team member's strengths, gaps, and development opportunities, and to align their professional development with the needs and goals of the project and the organization.

- Encourage team members to take ownership of their own professional development and growth, by setting their own learning goals, seeking out development opportunities, and tracking and reporting on their progress and accomplishments.

2. **Provide diverse and relevant learning and development opportunities**
   - Offer a variety of learning and development opportunities that cater to different learning styles, preferences, and needs, such as online courses, webinars, podcasts, books, or mentoring and coaching programs.
   - Ensure that the learning and development opportunities are relevant and applicable to the team members' roles, responsibilities, and career goals, and that they align with the project and organizational priorities and strategies.
   - Encourage team members to share their learning experiences and insights with each other, through peer learning groups, brown bag sessions, or knowledge-sharing platforms, to foster a culture of continuous learning and collaboration.

3. **Assign stretch assignments and development projects**
   - Provide team members with opportunities to take on new and challenging assignments or projects that stretch their skills and capabilities, and that expose them to new areas of the business or industry.

- Ensure that the stretch assignments and development projects are meaningful, impactful, and aligned with the team members' career goals and aspirations, and that they provide opportunities for growth, recognition, and advancement.
- Provide guidance, feedback, and support to help team members succeed in their stretch assignments and development projects, and celebrate their achievements and lessons learned.

4. Foster a culture of feedback, coaching, and mentoring
- Establish a regular cadence of feedback and coaching conversations with each team member, to provide ongoing guidance, support, and development in their roles and careers.
- Use a variety of feedback and coaching techniques, such as the SBI (situation, behavior, impact) model, the GROW (goal, reality, options, way forward) framework, or appreciative inquiry, to help team members identify their strengths, areas for improvement, and development opportunities.
- Encourage team members to seek out mentors or coaches, either within or outside the organization, who can provide guidance, advice, and support in their professional development and growth, and who can help them navigate challenges and opportunities in their careers.

5. Invest in training and certification programs
- Provide financial and logistical support for team members to attend training and certification programs

- that are relevant and valuable to their roles and careers, such as technical skills training, leadership development programs, or professional certification courses.
- Ensure that the training and certification programs are high-quality, reputable, and aligned with industry standards and best practices, and that they provide tangible benefits and outcomes for the team members and the organization.
- Recognize and celebrate team members who complete training and certification programs, and leverage their new skills and knowledge to enhance the team's capabilities and performance.

6. Support career advancement and mobility
- Provide team members with opportunities for career advancement and mobility, both within the project team and across the organization, based on their skills, interests, and aspirations.
- Use tools such as career path frameworks, job families, or talent review processes to identify and develop high-potential team members, and to create succession plans and development plans for key roles and positions.
- Encourage team members to explore and pursue career opportunities that align with their strengths, passions, and values, and that contribute to the overall success and impact of the organization.

Supporting professional development and growth in a remote project setting requires a proactive, personalized, and holistic approach that takes into account each team member's unique needs, goals, and circumstances.

It involves creating a learning culture that values and supports continuous growth and development, providing diverse and relevant learning and development opportunities, assigning stretch assignments and development projects, fostering a culture of feedback, coaching, and mentoring, investing in training and certification programs, and supporting career advancement and mobility.

To overcome the challenges of supporting professional development and growth in a remote setting, project managers can use a variety of strategies, such as:

- Leveraging technology and digital platforms, such as learning management systems, e-learning courses, or virtual coaching and mentoring programs, to provide accessible and flexible learning and development opportunities for remote team members.
- Encouraging team members to take initiative and ownership of their own professional development and growth, by setting learning goals, seeking out development opportunities, and sharing their progress and insights with their manager and peers.
- Building a strong network of mentors, coaches, and subject matter experts, both within and outside the organization, who can provide guidance, support, and expertise to remote team members in their professional development and growth.
- Continuously monitoring and evaluating the effectiveness and impact of professional development and growth initiatives, using metrics such as skills acquisition, engagement, retention, and promotion rates, and using

- this data to make data-driven decisions and adjustments to the initiatives and approaches.

By supporting professional development and growth in a remote project setting, project managers can create a team environment that is dynamic, innovative, and high-performing, where team members are able to realize their full potential and contribute to the success of the project and the organization. When team members feel supported, challenged, and valued in their professional development and growth, they are more likely to be engaged, committed, and loyal to their work and to the organization, and to bring their best selves and ideas to the table.

So if you're a remote project manager, make supporting professional development and growth a top priority. Assess team members' skills, interests, and aspirations, provide diverse and relevant learning and development opportunities, assign stretch assignments and development projects, foster a culture of feedback, coaching, and mentoring, invest in training and certification programs, and support career advancement and mobility. By investing in your team members' professional development and growth, you'll be well-equipped to build a remote team that is high-performing, engaged, and successful, and that can adapt and thrive in the face of change and uncertainty.

Part IV
Mastering the Art of Remote Leadership

Chapter 10
Adapting Your Leadership Style for Remote Work

Understanding Different Leadership Styles

As a remote project manager, mastering the art of remote leadership is essential for effectively guiding and supporting your team towards success. Remote leadership requires a unique set of skills, strategies, and mindsets that differ from traditional in-person leadership. One critical aspect of remote leadership is understanding and adapting your leadership style to the remote work environment and the needs of your team members.

Leadership style refers to the way in which a leader influences, motivates, and directs their team members to achieve common goals. There are several different leadership styles, each with its own strengths, weaknesses, and applications. Here are some of the most common leadership styles:

1. Autocratic leadership
- Autocratic leaders make decisions unilaterally, without seeking input or feedback from their team members.

- They provide clear direction and expectations, and expect their team members to follow orders and comply with rules and procedures.
- Autocratic leadership can be effective in high-pressure or crisis situations, or when quick decisions need to be made, but it can also lead to low morale, creativity, and engagement among team members.

2. **Democratic leadership**
- Democratic leaders involve their team members in the decision-making process, seeking their input, feedback, and ideas.
- They encourage open communication, collaboration, and participation, and value diversity of thought and perspective.
- Democratic leadership can lead to higher levels of engagement, ownership, and innovation among team members, but it can also be time-consuming and lead to delays in decision-making.

3. **Laissez-faire leadership**
- Laissez-faire leaders provide minimal direction, oversight, or feedback to their team members, allowing them to work independently and make their own decisions.
- They trust their team members to be self-motivated, resourceful, and accountable for their own work and results.
- Laissez-faire leadership can be effective with highly skilled and experienced team members, but it can also lead to lack of clarity, consistency, and accountability.

4. Transformational leadership
- Transformational leaders inspire and motivate their team members to achieve extraordinary results, by appealing to their values, emotions, and aspirations.
- They create a compelling vision and purpose for the team, and empower their team members to take ownership and initiative in achieving the vision.
- Transformational leadership can lead to high levels of engagement, creativity, and performance among team members, but it requires strong communication, charisma, and emotional intelligence skills.

5. Servant leadership
- Servant leaders prioritize the needs and development of their team members above their own, and focus on empowering and supporting their team members to succeed.
- They lead by example, demonstrating humility, empathy, and integrity, and creating a culture of trust, collaboration, and continuous improvement.
- Servant leadership can lead to high levels of loyalty, commitment, and growth among team members, but it requires a selfless and people-oriented mindset and skillset.

6. Situational leadership
- Situational leaders adapt their leadership style and approach based on the specific situation, task, and team members involved.

- They assess the readiness, ability, and motivation of their team members, and provide the appropriate level of direction, support, and autonomy to help them succeed.
- Situational leadership can be effective in dynamic and complex environments, but it requires flexibility, adaptability, and strong diagnostic and communication skills.

In a remote work setting, project managers may need to adapt their leadership style to account for the unique challenges and opportunities of remote collaboration and communication. For example, remote leaders may need to:
- Provide more frequent and clear communication and expectations, to compensate for the lack of face-to-face interaction and nonverbal cues.
- Foster a culture of trust, autonomy, and accountability, to empower remote team members to work independently and make decisions.
- Use technology and digital tools to facilitate collaboration, knowledge sharing, and social connection among remote team members.
- Demonstrate empathy, emotional intelligence, and cultural sensitivity, to build strong relationships and understanding with remote team members from diverse backgrounds and locations.

Ultimately, the most effective remote leadership style depends on the specific context, goals, and team members involved. Remote project managers need to be adaptable, responsive, and attuned to the needs and preferences of their team members, and willing to adjust their leadership style accordingly.

To master the art of remote leadership, project managers can use a variety of strategies, such as:

- Conducting a self-assessment of their own leadership style, strengths, and areas for improvement, using tools such as the Myers-Briggs Type Indicator, the DiSC profile, or the Leadership Practices Inventory.
- Seeking feedback and input from their team members and stakeholders on their leadership effectiveness and impact, using surveys, focus groups, or 360-degree feedback processes.
- Providing training and resources on remote leadership best practices and techniques, such as virtual communication, collaboration, and team-building, to their team members and peers.
- Building a strong network of mentors, coaches, and peers who can provide guidance, support, and accountability in their remote leadership journey.

By understanding and adapting their leadership style for remote work, project managers can create a team environment that is engaged, productive, and resilient, and that can thrive in the face of the unique challenges and opportunities of remote work. When remote team members feel supported, empowered, and valued by their leader, they are more likely to bring their best selves and ideas to the work, and to achieve outstanding results for the project and the organization.

So if you're a remote project manager, make mastering the art of remote leadership a top priority. Understand different leadership styles, assess your own leadership strengths and areas for improvement, seek feedback and input from your team members and stakeholders, provide training and resources on remote leadership best practices, and build a strong network of support and accountability. By investing in your own remote leadership skills and mindset, you'll be well-equipped to lead a remote team that is high-performing, engaged, and successful, and that can navigate the challenges and opportunities of the remote work landscape with confidence and agility.

Adjusting Your Approach for Virtual Teams

Leading virtual teams requires a different approach than leading in-person teams. Remote work presents unique challenges and opportunities that demand a tailored leadership style and strategy. As a remote project manager, it's essential to adjust your approach to account for the specific needs, preferences, and dynamics of your virtual team members, and to create an environment that fosters trust, collaboration, and high performance.

Here are some key ways in which you may need to adjust your approach for leading virtual teams:

1. **Emphasize communication and clarity**
   - In a virtual setting, communication can be more challenging and prone to misunderstandings, due to the lack of face-to-face interaction and nonverbal cues.
   - As a remote leader, you need to prioritize frequent, clear, and consistent communication with your team members, using a variety of channels and formats, such as video conferencing, instant messaging, email, or project management tools.
   - You also need to provide clear expectations, goals, and guidelines for your team members, and ensure that everyone understands their roles, responsibilities, and deadlines.

2. **Foster trust and psychological safety**
   - Trust and psychological safety are critical foundations for effective virtual teamwork, as they enable team members to take risks, share ideas, and collaborate openly and honestly.
   - As a remote leader, you need to actively build and maintain trust with your team members, by demonstrating reliability, integrity, and empathy, and by following through on your commitments and promises.
   - You also need to create a safe and inclusive environment where team members feel comfortable expressing their thoughts, feelings, and concerns, without fear of judgment, criticism, or retaliation.

3. **Empower autonomy and flexibility**
   - Virtual team members often value and thrive on autonomy and flexibility, as they can work from anywhere, at any time, and in their own preferred way.
   - As a remote leader, you need to empower your team members to take ownership and make decisions about their work, while providing guidance, support, and accountability as needed.
   - You also need to be flexible and adaptable in your leadership approach, recognizing that different team members may have different work styles, preferences, and needs, and adjusting your expectations and support accordingly.

4. **Promote collaboration and knowledge sharing**
Collaboration and knowledge sharing can be more challenging in a virtual setting, as team members may be working in silos or across different time zones and locations.

- As a remote leader, you need to actively promote and facilitate collaboration and knowledge sharing among your team members, by creating opportunities for teamwork, peer learning, and cross-functional projects.
- You also need to provide the necessary tools, resources, and training to enable effective virtual collaboration, such as project management software, knowledge management systems, or virtual whiteboarding tools.

5. Focus on results and outcomes
- In a virtual setting, it can be harder to monitor and manage team members' day-to-day activities and behaviors, as you can't see them working in person.
- As a remote leader, you need to shift your focus from managing tasks and time to managing results and outcomes, by setting clear goals, metrics, and deliverables, and holding team members accountable for achieving them.
- You also need to provide regular feedback, recognition, and support to help team members stay on track and improve their performance, using data-driven insights and evidence-based practices.

6. Prioritize well-being and work-life balance
- Virtual work can blur the boundaries between work and personal life, leading to stress, burnout, and disengagement among team members.
- As a remote leader, you need to prioritize the well-being and work-life balance of your team members, by encouraging healthy habits, such as regular breaks, exercise, and social connection, and by modeling these behaviors yourself.

- You also need to be sensitive and responsive to the unique challenges and pressures that virtual team members may face, such as isolation, distractions, or family responsibilities, and provide appropriate support and accommodations.

Adjusting your approach for leading virtual teams requires a mindset shift and a willingness to experiment, learn, and adapt. It involves recognizing and leveraging the unique strengths and opportunities of virtual work, while mitigating and addressing its challenges and limitations.

To effectively adjust your approach for virtual teams, you can use a variety of strategies, such as:

- Conducting regular check-ins and surveys with your team members to assess their needs, preferences, and feedback, and using this data to inform your leadership approach and decisions.
- Investing in your own learning and development as a remote leader, by attending webinars, reading books and articles, and seeking mentorship and coaching from experienced remote leaders.
- Experimenting with different leadership styles, techniques, and tools, and assessing their impact and effectiveness on your team's performance, engagement, and well-being.
- Building a strong network of peers, partners, and stakeholders who can provide guidance, support, and accountability in your remote leadership journey, and who can help you navigate the challenges and opportunities of virtual work.

By adjusting your approach for virtual teams, you can create a team environment that is agile, resilient, and high-performing, and that can thrive in the face of the unique challenges and opportunities of remote work. When virtual team members feel supported, empowered, and valued by their leader, they are more likely to bring their best selves and ideas to the work, and to achieve outstanding results for the project and the organization.

So if you're a remote project manager, make adjusting your approach for virtual teams a top priority. Emphasize communication and clarity, foster trust and psychological safety, empower autonomy and flexibility, promote collaboration and knowledge sharing, focus on results and outcomes, and prioritize well-being and work-life balance. By adapting your leadership approach to the specific needs and dynamics of your virtual team, you'll be well-equipped to lead a remote team that is engaged, productive, and successful, and that can navigate the challenges and opportunities of the remote work landscape with confidence and agility.

Balancing Direction and Autonomy

As a remote project manager, one of the key challenges and opportunities of leading virtual teams is finding the right balance between providing direction and granting autonomy to your team members. On one hand, virtual team members often value and thrive on the flexibility and independence that remote work affords them, and may resist or disengage if they feel micromanaged or constrained. On the other hand, virtual work can also create ambiguity, isolation, and lack of accountability, which can lead to missed deadlines, poor quality, or misaligned priorities if not properly managed.

Balancing direction and autonomy means finding the sweet spot where you provide enough guidance, support, and oversight to ensure that your team members are aligned, productive, and accountable, while also empowering them to make decisions, take ownership, and bring their unique skills and perspectives to the work. It involves adapting your leadership style and approach based on the specific needs, abilities, and preferences of your team members, and creating a culture of trust, transparency, and continuous improvement.

Here are some key strategies for balancing direction and autonomy in a remote project setting:

1. **Set clear goals and expectations**
   - Provide clear, specific, and measurable goals and expectations for your team members, in terms of what needs to be done, by when, and to what standard of quality.

- Ensure that these goals and expectations are aligned with the overall project objectives and organizational priorities, and that they are realistic, achievable, and motivating for your team members.
- Communicate these goals and expectations regularly and consistently, using a variety of channels and formats, such as project charters, kick-off meetings, status reports, or one-on-one check-ins.

2. Empower decision-making and problem-solving
- Give your team members the authority and autonomy to make decisions and solve problems related to their work, within the parameters of the project goals and expectations.
- Encourage them to use their skills, knowledge, and creativity to find innovative solutions and approaches, and to take calculated risks and learn from their mistakes.
- Provide them with the necessary tools, resources, and support to enable effective decision-making and problem-solving, such as access to information, training, or mentorship.

3. Establish clear roles and responsibilities
- Define clear roles and responsibilities for each team member, in terms of what they are accountable for delivering, and how their work fits into the overall project plan and team structure.
- Ensure that these roles and responsibilities are aligned with each team member's skills, interests, and development goals, and that they provide opportunities for growth, challenge, and recognition.

- Communicate these roles and responsibilities regularly and consistently, using tools such as RACI matrices, job descriptions, or performance agreements.

4. **Provide regular feedback and coaching**
   - Give your team members regular, timely, and constructive feedback on their performance, progress, and development, using a variety of methods and channels, such as one-on-one meetings, written comments, or 360-degree reviews.
   - Focus your feedback on specific behaviors, outcomes, and areas for improvement, rather than on personal traits or assumptions, and provide concrete examples and suggestions for how to improve.
   - Use coaching techniques, such as active listening, powerful questioning, and goal-setting, to help your team members identify their strengths, challenges, and aspirations, and to develop action plans for achieving their goals.

5. **Foster a culture of transparency and accountability**
   - Create a team culture that values and promotes transparency, honesty, and accountability, where team members feel safe and encouraged to share their progress, challenges, and feedback openly and proactively.
   - Model these behaviors yourself, by being open and transparent about your own work, decisions, and development, and by holding yourself accountable for your commitments and results.

- Use tools and processes, such as project dashboards, status reports, or retrospectives, to create visibility and accountability for team performance and outcomes, and to identify areas for improvement and learning.

6. **Adapt your approach based on individual needs and preferences**
   - Recognize that different team members may have different needs, preferences, and working styles when it comes to direction and autonomy, and adapt your leadership approach accordingly.
   - Some team members may prefer more structure, guidance, and check-ins, while others may thrive on more independence, flexibility, and space to experiment and innovate.
   - Use tools and techniques, such as personality assessments, learning style inventories, or one-on-one discussions, to understand and accommodate these individual differences, while still maintaining consistency and fairness across the team.

Balancing direction and autonomy is an ongoing process that requires regular reflection, adjustment, and communication. It involves being attuned to the changing needs and dynamics of your team and project, and being willing to adapt your leadership style and approach as needed to optimize performance, engagement, and well-being.

To effectively balance direction and autonomy, you can use a variety of strategies, such as:

- Conducting regular pulse checks and surveys to assess your team members' perceptions of direction and autonomy, and using this data to inform your leadership decisions and actions.
- Seeking feedback and input from your team members on how you can better support their needs for direction and autonomy, and being open and responsive to their suggestions and concerns.
- Experimenting with different leadership styles and techniques, such as situational leadership, servant leadership, or transformational leadership, and assessing their impact and effectiveness on team performance and satisfaction.
- Building a network of mentors, coaches, and peers who can provide guidance, support, and accountability in your journey to balance direction and autonomy, and who can help you navigate the challenges and opportunities of remote leadership.

By balancing direction and autonomy, you can create a team environment that is empowering, engaging, and high-performing, where team members feel trusted, supported, and motivated to bring their best selves and ideas to the work. When virtual team members have the right combination of guidance and independence, they are more likely to take ownership, innovate, and deliver outstanding results for the project and the organization.

So if you're a remote project manager, make balancing direction and autonomy a top priority. Set clear goals and expectations, empower decision-making and problem-solving, establish clear roles and responsibilities, provide regular feedback and coaching, foster a culture of transparency and accountability, and adapt your approach based on individual needs and preferences. By finding the sweet spot between direction and autonomy, you'll be well-equipped to lead a remote team that is engaged, productive, and successful, and that can thrive in the face of the unique challenges and opportunities of remote work.

Cultivating a Growth Mindset

In today's fast-paced and ever-changing business environment, cultivating a growth mindset is essential for remote project managers to lead their teams effectively and drive continuous improvement and innovation. A growth mindset is the belief that one's abilities, skills, and intelligence can be developed and expanded through dedication, hard work, and learning from challenges and setbacks. In contrast, a fixed mindset is the belief that one's abilities and traits are inherent and unchangeable, leading to a fear of failure, resistance to change, and limited growth and potential.

As a remote project manager, cultivating a growth mindset in yourself and your team members can have numerous benefits, such as:

- Enhancing resilience, adaptability, and problem-solving skills in the face of challenges and uncertainties
- Fostering a culture of continuous learning, experimentation, and innovation
- Encouraging collaboration, feedback-seeking, and knowledge-sharing among team members
- Promoting a sense of ownership, accountability, and empowerment for personal and professional development
- Improving team performance, engagement, and well-being by focusing on progress, effort, and growth rather than perfection or comparison

1. Embrace challenges and failures as opportunities for learning and growth
- View challenges, setbacks, and failures as natural and inevitable parts of the learning and growth process, rather than as threats or indicators of inadequacy.
- Encourage your team members to take on challenging projects, stretch assignments, and calculated risks, and to see them as opportunities to develop new skills, knowledge, and perspectives.
- When faced with failures or mistakes, focus on the lessons learned, the insights gained, and the actions to take to improve and move forward, rather than on blaming, shaming, or avoiding responsibility.

2. Emphasize effort, progress, and process over innate talent or intelligence
- Recognize and praise your team members for their hard work, persistence, and improvement, rather than for their innate abilities or intelligence.
- Use language and feedback that focuses on the process and strategies used, rather than on the person or the outcome, such as "I noticed how you broke down the problem into smaller steps and sought input from others" instead of "You're so smart!"
- Encourage your team members to set learning goals and track their progress over time, rather than just focusing on performance goals or external rewards.

3. **Foster a culture of continuous learning and development**
- Create opportunities and resources for your team members to learn new skills, gain new knowledge, and explore new areas of interest, such as through training, mentoring, or cross-functional projects.
- Encourage your team members to seek out feedback, ask questions, and share their knowledge and insights with others, and model these behaviors yourself.
- Celebrate and reward learning, experimentation, and risk-taking, even if they don't always lead to success, and frame failures as valuable data points and opportunities for growth.

4. **Promote a growth mindset through language, feedback, and recognition**
- Use language and feedback that emphasizes growth, possibility, and learning, rather than fixed traits or limitations, such as "not yet" instead of "can't", or "room for improvement" instead of "weakness".
- Provide specific, actionable, and forward-looking feedback that helps your team members identify their strengths, areas for growth, and next steps, rather than just evaluating their past performance.
- Recognize and celebrate your team members' growth mindset behaviors and achievements, such as taking on new challenges, learning from mistakes, or helping others grow, through public praise, rewards, or development opportunities.

5. Model a growth mindset in your own leadership and behavior
- Demonstrate a willingness to learn, experiment, and take risks yourself, and share your own learning journey and challenges with your team members.
- Seek out feedback and input from your team members and stakeholders on your own leadership and performance, and use it to identify areas for improvement and growth.
- Admit your own mistakes, uncertainties, and vulnerabilities, and model how to learn from them and move forward with resilience and optimism.

6. Create a psychologically safe and supportive environment for growth and learning
- Foster a team culture that values and promotes psychological safety, trust, and inclusion, where team members feel comfortable taking risks, expressing opinions, and asking for help without fear of judgment or retaliation.
- Provide support, resources, and accommodations for team members who may face challenges or barriers to growth and learning, such as flexible work arrangements, assistive technologies, or mentorship programs.
- Encourage and facilitate peer support, collaboration, and knowledge-sharing among team members, and create opportunities for them to learn from and inspire each other's growth and development.

Cultivating a growth mindset is an ongoing process that requires intentional effort, self-awareness, and adaptability from remote project managers and their teams. It involves challenging one's assumptions, embracing discomfort and uncertainty, and reframing challenges and setbacks as opportunities for learning and growth.

To effectively cultivate a growth mindset, remote project managers can use a variety of tools and techniques, such as:

Here are some key strategies for cultivating a growth mindset as a remote project manager:
- Using assessments and surveys, such as the Mindset Assessment Profile or the Strengths Finder, to identify and leverage team members' growth mindset traits and strengths.
- Providing training and resources on growth mindset concepts, techniques, and best practices, such as through workshops, webinars, or book clubs.
- Encouraging team members to set and track their own learning and development goals, and providing regular check-ins and feedback to support their progress and growth.
- Creating a team charter or manifesto that articulates the team's shared values, norms, and behaviors around growth mindset, learning, and innovation.
- Celebrating and showcasing team members' growth mindset achievements and stories, such as through a team newsletter, blog, or social media campaign.

By cultivating a growth mindset, remote project managers can create a team culture that is resilient, adaptable, and innovative, and that can thrive in the face of the complex and dynamic challenges of remote work. When team members believe in their own and others' potential for growth and development, they are more likely to take ownership of their learning, collaborate and support each other, and achieve outstanding results for the project and the organization.

So if you're a remote project manager, make cultivating a growth mindset a top priority for yourself and your team. Embrace challenges and failures as opportunities for learning and growth, emphasize effort and progress over innate talent, foster a culture of continuous learning and development, promote a growth mindset through language and feedback, model a growth mindset in your own leadership, and create a psychologically safe and supportive environment for growth and learning. By nurturing a growth mindset, you'll be well-equipped to lead a remote team that is resilient, adaptable, and innovative, and that can thrive in the face of the unique challenges and opportunities of remote work.

Chapter 11
Navigating Challenges and Conflicts

Identifying and Addressing Common Remote Work Challenges

As a remote project manager, navigating challenges and conflicts is an inevitable part of leading virtual teams. Remote work presents unique challenges and stressors that can impact team performance, communication, and well-being, such as isolation, technology issues, work-life balance, and cultural differences. Identifying and addressing these common remote work challenges proactively and effectively is essential for maintaining team productivity, engagement, and morale, and for preventing or resolving conflicts and issues that may arise.

Here are some of the most common remote work challenges that project managers may face, along with strategies for identifying and addressing them:

1. **Communication breakdowns and misunderstandings**
   - Remote communication can be more prone to misinterpretation, ambiguity, and delays, due to the lack of nonverbal cues, in-person interaction, and immediate feedback.
   - To identify communication challenges, look for signs such as unclear or inconsistent messages, long response times, or frequent misunderstandings or conflicts among team members.

- To address communication challenges, establish clear communication protocols and norms, such as using video conferencing for complex or sensitive discussions, following up verbal conversations with written summaries, or using project management tools to track and document decisions and actions.

2. Isolation and disconnection from the team and organization
- Remote team members may feel isolated, disconnected, or invisible, due to the lack of casual interactions, social support, and visibility that come with in-person work.
- To identify isolation and disconnection challenges, look for signs such as low participation in team meetings or events, lack of informal communication or relationship-building, or expressions of loneliness, anxiety, or disengagement.
- To address isolation and disconnection challenges, create opportunities for virtual social connection and team-building, such as coffee chats, happy hours, or interest groups, and provide regular check-ins and feedback to ensure that team members feel seen, heard, and valued.

3. Technology issues and limitations
- Remote work relies heavily on technology for communication, collaboration, and productivity, which can create challenges such as connectivity issues, software incompatibility, or cybersecurity risks.
- To identify technology challenges, look for signs such as frequent technical difficulties or delays, inconsistent use of tools or platforms, or complaints about the quality or reliability of technology.

- To address technology challenges, provide training and support on the use of remote work tools and best practices, establish backup plans and redundancies for critical systems, and invest in reliable and secure technology infrastructure and services.

4. **Work-life balance and boundary management**
- Remote work can blur the boundaries between work and personal life, leading to challenges such as overwork, burnout, or family-work conflicts.
- To identify work-life balance challenges, look for signs such as long or irregular work hours, lack of breaks or time off, or expressions of stress, fatigue, or guilt about balancing work and personal responsibilities.
- To address work-life balance challenges, encourage and model healthy work habits and boundaries, such as setting clear start and end times, taking regular breaks and vacations, and communicating expectations and limitations around availability and responsiveness.

5. **Cultural differences and communication styles**
- Remote teams may include members from diverse cultural backgrounds and communication styles, which can create challenges such as misunderstandings, stereotyping, or exclusion.
- To identify cultural and communication challenges, look for signs such as language barriers, nonverbal miscues, or discomfort or tension in cross-cultural interactions.

- To address cultural and communication challenges, provide training and resources on intercultural competence and communication, create a team culture of inclusion and respect for diversity, and encourage open and curious dialogue about cultural differences and perspectives.

6. Lack of trust and accountability
- Remote work can create challenges for building trust and accountability among team members, due to the lack of in-person observation, feedback, and relationship-building.
- To identify trust and accountability challenges, look for signs such as missed deadlines, poor quality work, or lack of follow-through on commitments or feedback.
- To address trust and accountability challenges, establish clear roles, responsibilities, and expectations, provide regular feedback and recognition, and create a culture of transparency, ownership, and continuous improvement.

Navigating challenges and conflicts in remote work requires a proactive, empathetic, and flexible approach from project managers. It involves anticipating and identifying potential challenges before they escalate, communicating openly and frequently with team members and stakeholders, and adapting leadership and management strategies to the unique needs and contexts of remote work.

To effectively navigate challenges and conflicts, remote project managers can use a variety of tools and techniques, such as:

- Conducting regular team and individual check-ins and surveys to assess team well-being, engagement, and satisfaction, and to identify and address any emerging challenges or conflicts.
- Providing training and resources on remote work best practices, such as communication, collaboration, and self-care, to equip team members with the skills and strategies to navigate remote work challenges.
- Encouraging and modeling a culture of psychological safety, trust, and open communication, where team members feel comfortable raising concerns, asking for help, and providing feedback and suggestions for improvement.
- Leveraging technology and tools, such as project management software, virtual whiteboards, or conflict resolution platforms, to facilitate communication, collaboration, and problem-solving in a remote setting.
- Seeking guidance and support from HR, IT, or other relevant functions, as well as from peers and mentors who have experience navigating remote work challenges and conflicts.

By effectively identifying and addressing common remote work challenges, remote project managers can create a team environment that is resilient, adaptable, and high-performing, even in the face of the unique stressors and uncertainties of remote work.

When team members feel supported, empowered, and equipped to navigate the challenges of remote work, they are more likely to maintain their productivity, engagement, and well-being, and to contribute to the overall success of the project and the organization.

So if you're a remote project manager, make navigating challenges and conflicts a top priority. Identify and address common remote work challenges, such as communication breakdowns, isolation and disconnection, technology issues, work-life balance, cultural differences, and lack of trust and accountability. Use a proactive, empathetic, and flexible approach, and leverage tools and techniques such as regular check-ins, training and resources, psychological safety, technology and tools, and guidance and support. By effectively navigating the challenges and conflicts of remote work, you'll be well-equipped to lead a remote team that is resilient, adaptable, and successful, and that can thrive in the face of the unique demands and opportunities of remote work.

Resolving Conflicts and Disagreements

Conflicts and disagreements are a natural and inevitable part of any team, including remote teams. They can arise from a variety of sources, such as differences in communication styles, work habits, values, or personalities, as well as from the unique challenges and stressors of remote work, such as isolation, technology issues, or work-life balance. As a remote project manager, effectively resolving conflicts and disagreements is essential for maintaining team cohesion, productivity, and well-being, and for preventing small issues from escalating into larger problems that can derail the project or damage relationships.

Here are some key strategies for resolving conflicts and disagreements in a remote project setting:

1. **Identify and acknowledge the conflict or disagreement**
   - Pay attention to signs of conflict or disagreement, such as tense or avoidant communication, missed deadlines, or decreased engagement or morale.
   - Acknowledge the conflict or disagreement openly and neutrally, without assigning blame or taking sides, and express your commitment to resolving it in a constructive and collaborative way.
   - Encourage team members to share their perspectives and concerns honestly and respectfully, and create a safe and nonjudgmental space for dialogue and problem-solving.

2. **Seek to understand the underlying issues and needs**
   - Ask open-ended questions and use active listening skills to understand each team member's perspective, feelings, and needs, and to identify any underlying issues or misunderstandings that may be contributing to the conflict or disagreement.
   - Avoid making assumptions or jumping to conclusions, and seek to clarify and validate each team member's experience and point of view, even if you don't agree with it.
   - Look for common ground and shared interests among team members, and focus on finding solutions that meet everyone's needs and goals, rather than on assigning blame or proving who is right or wrong.

3. **Brainstorm and evaluate potential solutions**
   - Encourage team members to brainstorm potential solutions or compromises that could resolve the conflict or disagreement, and to think creatively and openly about different options and approaches.
   - Evaluate each potential solution based on its feasibility, impact, and alignment with the project goals and values, and seek to find a solution that is mutually acceptable and beneficial to all parties involved.
   - Be willing to consider unconventional or innovative solutions, such as redefining roles or responsibilities, changing work processes or tools, or seeking outside mediation or support.

4. **Communicate the resolution and action plan**
   - Once a resolution or solution has been agreed upon, communicate it clearly and concisely to all team members involved, and ensure that everyone understands their roles, responsibilities, and expectations moving forward.
   - Develop an action plan that outlines the specific steps, timelines, and resources needed to implement the resolution, and assign clear ownership and accountability for each task or deliverable.
   - Follow up regularly with team members to ensure that the resolution is being implemented effectively, and to address any new issues or concerns that may arise.

5. **Provide ongoing support and feedback**
   - Recognize and appreciate team members' efforts and progress in resolving the conflict or disagreement, and provide ongoing support and encouragement to maintain the positive momentum and relationships.
   - Provide regular feedback and coaching to team members to help them develop their conflict resolution and communication skills, and to identify any areas for improvement or growth.
   - Model and reinforce a culture of open communication, collaboration, and continuous improvement, where conflicts and disagreements are seen as opportunities for learning and growth, rather than as threats or failures.

6. **Learn from the experience and prevent future conflicts**
   - After the conflict or disagreement has been resolved, take time to reflect on the experience and identify any lessons learned or best practices that can be applied to future situations.

- Seek feedback from team members on how the conflict resolution process could be improved or streamlined, and use this feedback to refine and adapt your approach and tools.
- Proactively identify and address any potential sources of future conflicts or disagreements, such as unclear roles or expectations, communication breakdowns, or resource constraints, and develop strategies and contingency plans to prevent or mitigate them.

Resolving conflicts and disagreements in a remote project setting requires a combination of empathy, communication, problem-solving, and leadership skills from project managers. It involves creating a psychologically safe and respectful environment for dialogue and collaboration, seeking to understand and address the underlying needs and interests of all parties involved, and finding mutually beneficial solutions that align with the project goals and values.

To effectively resolve conflicts and disagreements, remote project managers can use a variety of tools and techniques, such as:
- Using conflict resolution frameworks or models, such as the Thomas-Kilmann Conflict Mode Instrument or the Interest-Based Relational Approach, to assess and navigate different conflict styles and strategies.
- Leveraging virtual communication and collaboration tools, such as video conferencing, instant messaging, or shared documents, to facilitate open and respectful dialogue and problem-solving among team members.

- Providing training and resources on conflict resolution, communication, and emotional intelligence skills, to equip team members with the tools and strategies to navigate conflicts and disagreements effectively.
- Seeking guidance and support from HR, legal, or other relevant functions, as well as from peers and mentors who have experience resolving conflicts and disagreements in a remote setting.
- Celebrating and showcasing successful examples of conflict resolution and collaboration, to reinforce a culture of positive and constructive problem-solving and teamwork.

By effectively resolving conflicts and disagreements, remote project managers can create a team environment that is resilient, adaptable, and high-performing, even in the face of the unique challenges and stressors of remote work. When team members feel heard, respected, and empowered to navigate conflicts and disagreements in a constructive and collaborative way, they are more likely to maintain their engagement, productivity, and well-being, and to contribute to the overall success of the project and the organization.

So if you're a remote project manager, make resolving conflicts and disagreements a top priority. Identify and acknowledge conflicts and disagreements openly and neutrally, seek to understand the underlying issues and needs, brainstorm and evaluate potential solutions, communicate the resolution and action plan clearly and concisely, provide ongoing support and feedback, and learn from the experience and prevent future conflicts.

Use a combination of empathy, communication, problem-solving, and leadership skills, and leverage tools and techniques such as conflict resolution frameworks, virtual communication and collaboration tools, training and resources, guidance and support, and celebration and showcasing of success. By effectively resolving conflicts and disagreements, you'll be well-equipped to lead a remote team that is resilient, adaptable, and successful, and that can thrive in the face of the unique challenges and opportunities of remote work.

Managing Underperformance and Disciplinary Issues

As a remote project manager, managing underperformance and disciplinary issues is a critical part of ensuring team productivity, accountability, and morale. Underperformance refers to a situation where a team member is not meeting the expected standards of performance or behavior, while disciplinary issues refer to violations of company policies, procedures, or values that require corrective action. Managing these issues effectively is essential for maintaining team performance and trust, and for preventing small problems from escalating into larger ones that can damage the project or the team.

Here are some key strategies for managing underperformance and disciplinary issues in a remote project setting:

1. **Set clear expectations and standards**
   - Clearly communicate and document the expected standards of performance and behavior for each team member, including specific goals, metrics, and competencies, as well as the consequences of not meeting these standards.
   - Ensure that these expectations and standards are aligned with the project goals and values, and that they are realistic, achievable, and fair for all team members.
   - Provide regular feedback and coaching to team members to help them understand and meet these expectations and standards, and to identify any areas for improvement or development.

2. Identify and address underperformance early and objectively

- Regularly monitor and assess team members' performance and behavior, using objective data and metrics, as well as feedback from stakeholders and peers.
- If you identify any instances of underperformance, address them early and directly with the team member, using a non-judgmental and constructive approach that focuses on the specific behaviors or outcomes, rather than on the person.
- Seek to understand the root causes of the underperformance, such as lack of skills, resources, or motivation, and work with the team member to develop an action plan to address these issues and improve their performance.

3. Follow a fair and consistent disciplinary process

- If a team member's behavior or performance violates company policies, procedures, or values, follow a fair and consistent disciplinary process that is aligned with HR and legal guidelines, and that is communicated clearly to all team members.
- Gather and document all relevant facts and evidence related to the disciplinary issue, and conduct a thorough and impartial investigation that allows the team member to provide their perspective and explanation.
- Determine the appropriate level of disciplinary action based on the severity and frequency of the issue, as well as the team member's history and attitude, and communicate this action clearly and confidentially to the team member.

4. Provide support and resources for improvement
- After addressing underperformance or disciplinary issues, provide the team member with the necessary support and resources to help them improve their performance and behavior, and to meet the expected standards.
- This may include additional training, coaching, or mentoring, as well as clear goals, timelines, and feedback mechanisms to track their progress and development.
- Emphasize the importance of continuous improvement and growth, and encourage the team member to take ownership and initiative in their own development and performance.

5. Document and communicate decisions and actions
- Document all decisions and actions related to underperformance and disciplinary issues, including the specific behaviors or outcomes, the investigation process, the disciplinary action, and the improvement plan.
- Communicate these decisions and actions clearly and confidentially to the team member, as well as to any relevant stakeholders, such as HR, legal, or senior management, while respecting the team member's privacy and dignity.
- Ensure that all documentation and communication is accurate, objective, and consistent with company policies and procedures, and that it can withstand legal or ethical scrutiny if necessary.

6. Monitor and evaluate the impact and effectiveness

- After implementing the improvement plan and disciplinary action, regularly monitor and evaluate the team member's performance and behavior, and provide ongoing feedback and support to help them sustain and improve their performance.
- Assess the impact and effectiveness of the disciplinary process and improvement plan on the team member's performance and morale, as well as on the overall team and project performance and culture.
- Use this assessment to identify any lessons learned or best practices that can be applied to future situations, and to refine and improve the disciplinary and performance management processes and tools.

Managing underperformance and disciplinary issues in a remote project setting requires a combination of clear communication, fair and consistent processes, and supportive and developmental approaches from project managers. It involves setting clear expectations and standards, identifying and addressing issues early and objectively, following a fair and consistent disciplinary process, providing support and resources for improvement, documenting and communicating decisions and actions, and monitoring and evaluating the impact and effectiveness.

To effectively manage underperformance and disciplinary issues, remote project managers can use a variety of tools and techniques, such as:

- Using performance management software or tools, such as goal-setting and tracking apps, performance review templates, or disciplinary action forms, to document and communicate performance and disciplinary decisions and actions.
- Leveraging virtual communication and collaboration tools, such as video conferencing, instant messaging, or shared documents, to facilitate open and respectful dialogue and feedback with team members.
- Providing training and resources on performance management, coaching, and disciplinary processes, to equip team members and managers with the skills and strategies to navigate these situations effectively and fairly.
- Seeking guidance and support from HR, legal, or other relevant functions, as well as from peers and mentors who have experience managing underperformance and disciplinary issues in a remote setting.
- Creating a culture of accountability, transparency, and continuous improvement, where underperformance and disciplinary issues are seen as opportunities for learning and growth, rather than as punitive or demoralizing measures.

By effectively managing underperformance and disciplinary issues, remote project managers can create a team environment that is fair, consistent, and developmental, even in the face of the unique challenges and stressors of remote work. When team members feel supported, accountable, and empowered to improve their performance and behavior, they are more likely to maintain their engagement, productivity, and well-being, and to contribute to the overall success of the project and the organization.

So if you're a remote project manager, make managing underperformance and disciplinary issues a top priority. Set clear expectations and standards, identify and address underperformance early and objectively, follow a fair and consistent disciplinary process, provide support and resources for improvement, document and communicate decisions and actions, and monitor and evaluate the impact and effectiveness. Use a combination of clear communication, fair and consistent processes, and supportive and developmental approaches, and leverage tools and techniques such as performance management software, virtual communication and collaboration tools, training and resources, guidance and support, and a culture of accountability and continuous improvement. By effectively managing underperformance and disciplinary issues, you'll be well-equipped to lead a remote team that is fair, consistent, and developmental, and that can thrive in the face of the unique challenges and opportunities of remote work.

Maintaining Team Morale and Engagement

In a remote project setting, maintaining team morale and engagement is a critical factor in driving team performance, collaboration, and well-being. Morale refers to the overall level of satisfaction, enthusiasm, and confidence that team members feel about their work and their team, while engagement refers to the level of emotional and cognitive connection and commitment that team members have to their work and their organization. When team morale and engagement are high, team members are more likely to be productive, creative, and resilient, and to go above and beyond to achieve project goals and deliver high-quality results.

However, maintaining team morale and engagement in a remote setting can be challenging, due to factors such as isolation, communication barriers, work-life balance issues, and lack of in-person interaction and recognition. As a remote project manager, it's essential to actively and intentionally cultivate and sustain team morale and engagement, using a variety of strategies and techniques.

Here are some key strategies for maintaining team morale and engagement in a remote project setting:

1. **Foster a positive and supportive team culture**
   - Create a team culture that values and promotes positivity, respect, trust, and collaboration, and that encourages team members to support and appreciate each other's efforts and contributions.

- Model and reinforce positive behaviors and attitudes, such as gratitude, empathy, and humor, and discourage negative behaviors and attitudes, such as gossip, criticism, or cynicism.
- Celebrate team successes and milestones, and acknowledge and appreciate individual and team achievements, using a variety of recognition and reward methods, such as public praise, bonuses, or development opportunities.

2. **Communicate regularly and transparently**
- Establish regular and consistent communication channels and rhythms, such as daily check-ins, weekly team meetings, or monthly newsletters, to keep team members informed, aligned, and connected.
- Share project updates, goals, and challenges transparently and honestly, and seek team members' input and feedback on project decisions and directions.
- Use a variety of communication methods and styles, such as video, audio, or written, to cater to different preferences and needs, and to create a sense of personal connection and presence.

3. **Provide meaningful work and growth opportunities**
- Assign work and projects that are challenging, meaningful, and aligned with team members' strengths, interests, and development goals, and that provide opportunities for learning, growth, and impact.
- Encourage team members to take ownership and initiative in their work, and to propose and implement their own ideas and solutions for improving project processes and outcomes.

- Provide regular feedback, coaching, and mentoring to help team members develop their skills, knowledge, and careers, and to support their ongoing engagement and motivation.

4. Promote work-life balance and well-being
- Encourage and model healthy work-life balance and self-care practices, such as setting clear work hours and boundaries, taking regular breaks and time off, and engaging in physical, mental, and social activities outside of work.
- Provide resources and support for team members' well-being and resilience, such as wellness programs, employee assistance programs, or mental health resources.
- Be flexible and accommodating of team members' personal and family needs and circumstances, such as caregiving responsibilities, health issues, or time zone differences, and work with them to find mutually beneficial solutions and arrangements.

5. Foster social connection and team bonding
- Create opportunities for team members to connect and bond with each other on a personal and social level, such as virtual coffee chats, happy hours, or game nights.
- Encourage and facilitate peer-to-peer recognition and appreciation, such as shout-outs, kudos, or gift-giving, to build a sense of community and support among team members.

- Organize virtual team-building activities and events, such as trivia contests, escape rooms, or charity challenges, to foster collaboration, creativity, and fun, and to break up the monotony and isolation of remote work.

6. Seek and act on feedback and input

- Regularly seek and listen to team members' feedback and input on their work experience, morale, and engagement, using a variety of methods, such as surveys, focus groups, or one-on-one conversations.
- Act on the feedback and input in a timely and transparent manner, and communicate the actions and outcomes to the team, to demonstrate that their voices and needs are heard and valued.
- Continuously monitor and evaluate the impact and effectiveness of the morale and engagement strategies and techniques, and adjust and improve them based on the feedback and results.

Maintaining team morale and engagement in a remote project setting requires a proactive, empathetic, and adaptive approach from project managers. It involves creating a positive and supportive team culture, communicating regularly and transparently, providing meaningful work and growth opportunities, promoting work-life balance and well-being, fostering social connection and team bonding, and seeking and acting on feedback and input.

To effectively maintain team morale and engagement, remote project managers can use a variety of tools and techniques, such as:

- Using team collaboration and communication platforms, such as Slack, Microsoft Teams, or Zoom, to facilitate regular and engaging interactions and discussions among team members.
- Leveraging employee recognition and rewards programs, such as peer-to-peer recognition apps, gift cards, or customized swag, to celebrate and appreciate team members' contributions and achievements.
- Providing access to online learning and development resources, such as courses, webinars, or mentoring programs, to support team members' ongoing growth and engagement.
- Organizing virtual team-building and social activities, such as online escape rooms, trivia contests, or cooking classes, to create fun and bonding experiences for team members.
- Conducting regular pulse surveys and feedback sessions, such as using tools like TINYpulse or Culture Amp, to gather and act on team members' input and needs.

By effectively maintaining team morale and engagement, remote project managers can create a team environment that is positive, supportive, and motivating, even in the face of the unique challenges and stressors of remote work. When team members feel valued, connected, and empowered in their work and their team, they are more likely to be engaged, productive, and committed to the project and the organization, and to go above and beyond to achieve outstanding results.

So if you're a remote project manager, make maintaining team morale and engagement a top priority. Foster a positive and supportive team culture, communicate regularly and transparently, provide meaningful work and growth opportunities, promote work-life balance and well-being, foster social connection and team bonding, and seek and act on feedback and input. Use a proactive, empathetic, and adaptive approach, and leverage tools and techniques such as team collaboration and communication platforms, employee recognition and rewards programs, online learning and development resources, virtual team-building and social activities, and regular pulse surveys and feedback sessions. By effectively maintaining team morale and engagement, you'll be well-equipped to lead a remote team that is positive, supportive, and motivating, and that can thrive in the face of the unique challenges and opportunities of remote work.

Chapter 12
Promoting Work-Life Balance and Wellbeing

Encouraging Healthy Work Habits and Boundaries

In today's fast-paced and always-connected work environment, promoting work-life balance and well-being has become increasingly important, especially for remote teams. Work-life balance refers to the ability to effectively manage and prioritize work responsibilities and personal life commitments, while well-being refers to the overall physical, mental, and emotional health and happiness of individuals. When team members have a healthy work-life balance and well-being, they are more likely to be productive, engaged, and resilient, and to experience higher levels of job satisfaction and overall quality of life.

However, achieving work-life balance and well-being can be challenging in a remote work setting, due to factors such as blurred boundaries between work and personal life, lack of physical separation between work and home environments, and the pressure to be constantly available and responsive to work demands. As a remote project manager, it's essential to actively promote and support healthy work habits and boundaries, and to create a team culture that values and prioritizes work-life balance and well-being.

Here are some key strategies for encouraging healthy work habits and boundaries in a remote team:

1. **Set clear expectations and guidelines**
   - Clearly communicate and document the expected work hours, availability, and response times for team members, and ensure that these expectations are reasonable, realistic, and aligned with the project goals and timelines.
   - Encourage team members to set their own work schedules and routines that work best for their personal and family needs and preferences, while still meeting the project requirements and deadlines.
   - Establish guidelines and policies for after-hours or weekend work, vacation time, and sick leave, and ensure that these policies are fair, consistent, and applied equally to all team members.

2. **Model and reinforce healthy work habits and boundaries**
   - As a project manager, model healthy work habits and boundaries yourself, by setting and communicating your own work schedule and availability, taking regular breaks and time off, and avoiding work-related communication outside of work hours.
   - Reinforce and celebrate healthy work habits and boundaries among team members, by acknowledging and appreciating their efforts to prioritize their well-being and balance, and by discouraging or addressing any unhealthy or unsustainable work behaviors or expectations.
   - Create a team culture that values and supports work-life balance and well-being, by openly discussing and addressing any challenges or concerns, and by providing resources and support for team members to manage their workload and stress levels effectively.

3. **Encourage regular breaks and time off**
   - Encourage team members to take regular breaks throughout the workday, such as stepping away from their computer, stretching, or engaging in brief physical or mental activities, to recharge and refocus their energy and attention.
   - Promote the use of vacation time and personal days, and ensure that team members feel comfortable and supported in taking time off to rest, recharge, and attend to personal or family needs and commitments.
   - Consider implementing team-wide break or time-off policies, such as mandatory lunch breaks, no-meeting Fridays, or summer Fridays, to create a shared culture of rest and renewal, and to prevent burnout and overwork.

4. **Provide resources and support for well-being and stress management**
   - Offer and promote resources and support for team members' physical, mental, and emotional well-being, such as employee assistance programs, wellness programs, or mental health benefits.
   - Provide training and resources on stress management, resilience, and self-care techniques, such as mindfulness, exercise, or sleep hygiene, to help team members develop healthy coping strategies and habits.
   - Encourage and facilitate peer support and connection among team members, such as through virtual wellness groups, buddy systems, or mental health champions, to create a sense of community and shared support for well-being and balance.

5. **Prioritize and streamline workload and communication**
   - Regularly review and prioritize the team's workload and goals, and ensure that the workload is distributed fairly and realistically among team members, based on their skills, capacity, and availability.
   - Streamline and optimize communication and collaboration processes and tools, to reduce unnecessary or redundant meetings, emails, or notifications, and to create more focused and productive work time for team members.
   - Encourage team members to use tools and techniques for managing their time and tasks effectively, such as time blocking, task batching, or productivity apps, and provide training and support for using these tools and techniques effectively.

6. **Assess and adjust strategies and policies regularly**
   - Regularly assess and gather feedback from team members on their work-life balance and well-being, using surveys, interviews, or focus groups, to identify any challenges, concerns, or areas for improvement.
   - Use the feedback and data to adjust and refine the work-life balance and well-being strategies and policies, and to address any emerging issues or needs in a timely and effective manner.
   - Continuously communicate and reinforce the importance and value of work-life balance and well-being to the team and the organization, and celebrate and showcase any successes or best practices in promoting and supporting healthy work habits and boundaries.

Promoting work-life balance and well-being, and encouraging healthy work habits and boundaries, is a critical responsibility of remote project managers. It involves setting clear expectations and guidelines, modeling and reinforcing healthy behaviors, encouraging regular breaks and time off, providing resources and support for well-being and stress management, prioritizing and streamlining workload and communication, and regularly assessing and adjusting strategies and policies.

To effectively promote work-life balance and well-being, remote project managers can use a variety of tools and techniques, such as:

- Using time tracking and productivity tools, such as RescueTime or Toggl, to monitor and optimize team members' work patterns and habits, and to identify any areas for improvement or balance.
- Leveraging employee wellness and assistance programs, such as Headspace or Talkspace, to provide accessible and confidential resources and support for team members' mental and emotional well-being.
- Organizing virtual wellness and self-care activities and challenges, such as yoga classes, meditation sessions, or step challenges, to create fun and engaging opportunities for team members to prioritize their health and well-being.
- Conducting regular work-life balance and well-being surveys and assessments, such as using the Work-Life Balance Checklist or the Maslach Burnout Inventory, to gather data and insights on team members' experiences and needs.

- Creating and communicating clear policies and guidelines for work-life balance and well-being, such as through a team charter, employee handbook, or wellness manifesto, to establish a shared understanding and commitment to healthy work habits and boundaries.

By effectively promoting work-life balance and well-being, and encouraging healthy work habits and boundaries, remote project managers can create a team culture that values and supports the holistic health and happiness of team members. When team members feel empowered and supported to prioritize their well-being and balance, they are more likely to be engaged, productive, and committed to their work and their team, and to contribute to a positive and sustainable work environment.

So if you're a remote project manager, make promoting work-life balance and well-being a top priority. Set clear expectations and guidelines, model and reinforce healthy work habits and boundaries, encourage regular breaks and time off, provide resources and support for well-being and stress management, prioritize and streamline workload and communication, and assess and adjust strategies and policies regularly. Use tools and techniques such as time tracking and productivity tools, employee wellness and assistance programs, virtual wellness and self-care activities and challenges, regular work-life balance and well-being surveys and assessments, and clear policies and guidelines for work-life balance and well-being. By effectively promoting work-life balance and well-being, and encouraging healthy work habits and boundaries, you'll be well-equipped to lead a remote team that is healthy, happy, and thriving, and that can sustain high levels of performance and engagement over the long term.

Supporting Mental Health and Stress Management

Mental health and stress management are critical components of overall well-being and work-life balance, especially in the context of remote work. Mental health refers to a person's emotional, psychological, and social well-being, while stress management refers to the ability to effectively cope with and reduce the negative impacts of stress on one's health and performance. When team members have good mental health and stress management skills, they are more likely to be resilient, adaptable, and productive, and to experience higher levels of job satisfaction, creativity, and collaboration.

However, remote work can pose unique challenges and risks to mental health and stress management, such as social isolation, blurred work-life boundaries, increased screen time, and lack of access to traditional support systems and resources. As a remote project manager, it's essential to proactively support and promote mental health and stress management among your team members, and to create a team culture that values and prioritizes psychological safety, well-being, and self-care.

Here are some key strategies for supporting mental health and stress management in a remote team:

1. **Normalize and destigmatize mental health conversations**
- Create a team culture that normalizes and destigmatizes conversations about mental health and stress, by openly discussing and addressing these topics in team meetings, one-on-one check-ins, and other communication channels.

- Encourage team members to share their own experiences, challenges, and coping strategies related to mental health and stress, and to seek and offer support and resources to each other.
- Model vulnerability and authenticity in your own communication and behavior, by sharing your own struggles and strategies for managing stress and maintaining mental well-being, and by demonstrating empathy and non-judgment towards others' experiences and needs.

2. Provide access to mental health resources and support
- Offer and promote access to mental health resources and support, such as employee assistance programs (EAPs), teletherapy services, or mental health apps and tools, to help team members proactively manage their mental health and stress levels.
- Provide training and education on mental health and stress management topics, such as resilience, mindfulness, or cognitive-behavioral techniques, to equip team members with practical skills and strategies for coping with stress and promoting mental well-being.
- Consider offering mental health days or breaks, such as designated time off for self-care or wellness activities, to encourage team members to prioritize their mental health and prevent burnout and overwork.

3. Foster a sense of connection and belonging
Create opportunities for team members to connect and bond with each other on a personal and social level, such as through virtual team-building activities, interest groups, or buddy systems, to combat feelings of isolation and loneliness.

- Encourage and facilitate peer support and mentorship among team members, such as through mental health champions or peer support groups, to create a sense of community and shared understanding around mental health and stress.
- Celebrate and appreciate team members' unique strengths, contributions, and achievements, and create a team culture that values and promotes diversity, inclusion, and psychological safety.

4. **Promote work-life balance and boundary-setting**
- Encourage and model healthy work-life boundaries and habits, such as setting clear start and end times for work, taking regular breaks and time off, and avoiding work-related communication outside of work hours.
- Provide flexibility and autonomy for team members to manage their own work schedules and routines, based on their individual needs and preferences, while still meeting project goals and deadlines.
- Regularly assess and adjust workload and expectations to ensure that they are realistic, sustainable, and aligned with team members' capacity and well-being, and to prevent overwork and burnout.

5. **Monitor and address signs of stress and mental health concerns**
- Regularly check in with team members, both individually and as a group, to assess their stress levels, mental well-being, and any challenges or concerns they may be facing, using tools such as surveys, interviews, or mood tracking apps.

- Be attentive to and proactively address any signs of stress, anxiety, depression, or other mental health concerns among team members, such as changes in behavior, performance, or communication, and provide appropriate support and resources.
- Work with HR, leadership, and other relevant stakeholders to develop and implement policies and procedures for addressing and accommodating mental health needs and requests, such as leave of absence, reasonable accommodations, or return-to-work plans.

6. Cultivate a growth mindset and resilience
- Encourage and model a growth mindset and resilience among team members, by framing challenges and setbacks as opportunities for learning and growth, and by celebrating effort, progress, and improvement over perfection or outcomes.
- Provide opportunities for team members to develop and practice resilience skills, such as problem-solving, adaptability, or emotional regulation, through training, coaching, or stretch assignments.
- Foster a team culture that values and supports continuous learning, experimentation, and innovation, and that encourages team members to take calculated risks, learn from failures, and bounce back from adversity.

Supporting mental health and stress management in a remote team requires a proactive, empathetic, and holistic approach from project managers. It involves normalizing and destigmatizing mental health conversations, providing access to mental health resources and support, fostering a sense of connection and belonging, promoting work-life balance and boundary-setting, monitoring and addressing signs of stress and mental health concerns, and cultivating a growth mindset and resilience.

To effectively support mental health and stress management, remote project managers can use a variety of tools and techniques, such as:
- Using mental health and well-being platforms, such as Headspace, Calm, or Talkspace, to provide accessible and confidential resources and support for team members' mental health needs.
- Leveraging team communication and collaboration tools, such as Slack or Microsoft Teams, to create dedicated channels or groups for mental health and well-being discussions and resources.
- Organizing virtual mental health and stress management workshops, webinars, or challenges, such as mindfulness sessions, stress reduction techniques, or gratitude practices, to provide practical skills and strategies for team members.
- Conducting regular mental health and well-being check-ins and assessments, such as using the PHQ-9 or GAD-7 questionnaires, to monitor and address any signs of stress, anxiety, or depression among team members.
- Creating and communicating clear policies and guidelines for mental health and well-being support, such as through a mental health handbook, resource guide, or crisis plan, to establish a shared understanding and commitment to psychological safety and well-being.

By effectively supporting mental health and stress management in a remote team, project managers can create a team culture that values and prioritizes the psychological well-being and resilience of team members. When team members feel supported, understood, and empowered to manage their mental health and stress levels, they are more likely to be engaged, productive, and committed to their work and their team, and to contribute to a positive and sustainable work environment.

So if you're a remote project manager, make supporting mental health and stress management a top priority. Normalize and destigmatize mental health conversations, provide access to mental health resources and support, foster a sense of connection and belonging, promote work-life balance and boundary-setting, monitor and address signs of stress and mental health concerns, and cultivate a growth mindset and resilience. Use tools and techniques such as mental health and well-being platforms, team communication and collaboration tools, virtual mental health and stress management workshops and webinars, regular mental health and well-being check-ins and assessments, and clear policies and guidelines for mental health and well-being support. By effectively supporting mental health and stress management in your remote team, you'll be well-equipped to lead a team that is psychologically safe, resilient, and thriving, and that can sustain high levels of well-being and performance over the long term.

Recognizing Signs of Burnout and Overwork

Burnout and overwork are serious and prevalent issues in today's fast-paced and demanding work environment, especially for remote teams. Burnout is a state of chronic stress and exhaustion that leads to physical, emotional, and mental depletion, while overwork refers to the practice of working excessively long hours or taking on too many responsibilities, often at the expense of one's health, well-being, and personal life. When team members experience burnout or overwork, they are more likely to have decreased productivity, creativity, and engagement, as well as increased absenteeism, turnover, and health problems.

As a remote project manager, it's essential to be aware of and proactively recognize the signs of burnout and overwork among your team members, and to take appropriate steps to prevent, mitigate, and address these issues. By doing so, you can create a team culture that values and supports sustainable performance, well-being, and work-life balance, and that enables team members to bring their best selves and contributions to their work and their team.

Here are some common signs of burnout and overwork to look out for in your remote team members:

1. **Physical symptoms**
   - Chronic fatigue or exhaustion, even after rest or sleep
   - Frequent headaches, muscle tension, or other physical pain
   - Changes in appetite, weight, or sleep patterns

- Increased susceptibility to illnesses or infections

2. **Emotional symptoms**
   - Increased irritability, frustration, or anger
   - Decreased motivation, enthusiasm, or sense of purpose
   - Feelings of helplessness, hopelessness, or inadequacy
   - Emotional exhaustion or numbness

3. **Behavioral symptoms**
   - Procrastination or avoidance of work tasks or responsibilities
   - Decreased productivity, quality, or attention to detail
   - Increased absenteeism, tardiness, or presenteeism
   - Social withdrawal or isolation from team members or activities

4. **Cognitive symptoms**
   - Difficulty concentrating, remembering, or making decisions
   - Decreased creativity, problem-solving, or critical thinking skills
   - Negative or cynical attitudes towards work, colleagues, or oneself
   - Difficulty separating work from personal life or setting boundaries

5. **Work-related symptoms**
   - Consistently working long hours or overtime, even when not required or necessary
   - Taking on too many projects, tasks, or responsibilities, often with unrealistic deadlines or expectations

- Neglecting or sacrificing personal life, hobbies, or relationships for work
- Feeling pressured or obligated to be constantly available or responsive to work demands

If you notice any of these signs of burnout or overwork in your remote team members, it's important to take proactive and supportive steps to address and mitigate these issues. Here are some strategies for preventing and addressing burnout and overwork in your remote team:

1. Model and encourage sustainable work habits and boundaries
- Set clear expectations and guidelines for work hours, availability, and responsiveness, and model these behaviors yourself
- Encourage team members to take regular breaks, time off, and vacations, and to prioritize self-care and personal life activities
- Provide flexibility and autonomy for team members to manage their own work schedules and routines, based on their individual needs and preferences

2. Provide resources and support for well-being and stress management
- Offer and promote access to mental health resources and support, such as employee assistance programs, teletherapy services, or wellness apps and tools
- Provide training and education on stress management, resilience, and self-care techniques, such as mindfulness, exercise, or time management

- Encourage and facilitate peer support and connection among team members, such as through mental health champions, buddy systems, or virtual wellness activities

3. **Regularly assess and adjust workload and expectations**
   - Regularly review and prioritize team members' workload and responsibilities, and ensure that they are realistic, sustainable, and aligned with their capacity and well-being
   - Provide clear and reasonable deadlines and expectations for deliverables and projects, and avoid last-minute changes or additions
   - Be open to adjusting or reallocating workload or resources as needed, based on team members' feedback, performance, or well-being

4. **Foster a culture of open communication and psychological safety**
   - Encourage and model open and honest communication about workload, stress, and well-being, and create a safe and non-judgmental space for team members to share their experiences and needs
   - Regularly check in with team members, both individually and as a group, to assess their well-being, identify any challenges or concerns, and provide support and resources as needed
   - Foster a team culture that values and supports vulnerability, empathy, and mutual respect, and that promotes psychological safety and trust among team members

5. Celebrate and recognize sustainable performance and well-being

- Recognize and celebrate team members who demonstrate sustainable work habits, self-care practices, and work-life balance, and who contribute to a positive and supportive team culture
- Provide rewards and incentives for team members who prioritize their well-being and prevent burnout and overwork, such as wellness benefits, extra time off, or professional development opportunities
- Communicate the value and importance of sustainable performance and well-being to the team and the organization, and advocate for policies and practices that support these goals

Recognizing and addressing signs of burnout and overwork in a remote team requires ongoing attention, empathy, and proactivity from project managers. It involves being aware of and attuned to the physical, emotional, behavioral, cognitive, and work-related symptoms of burnout and overwork, and taking appropriate steps to prevent, mitigate, and address these issues.

To effectively recognize and address signs of burnout and overwork, remote project managers can use a variety of tools and techniques, such as:

- Using employee well-being and engagement surveys, such as the Maslach Burnout Inventory or the Utrecht Work Engagement Scale, to assess and monitor team members' levels of burnout, overwork, and well-being over time

- Leveraging project management and time tracking tools, such as Asana, Trello, or Toggl, to monitor and optimize team members' workload, productivity, and time allocation, and to identify any patterns or risks of overwork or burnout
- Providing access to mental health and well-being resources and support, such as employee assistance programs, wellness apps, or stress management training, to help team members proactively manage their stress levels and prevent burnout
- Encouraging and modeling sustainable work habits and boundaries, such as taking regular breaks, setting clear work hours, and prioritizing self-care and personal life activities, and communicating the value and importance of these practices to the team and the organization
- Fostering a culture of open communication, psychological safety, and mutual support, where team members feel comfortable and encouraged to share their experiences, challenges, and needs related to burnout and overwork, and to seek and provide support and resources to each other

By effectively recognizing and addressing signs of burnout and overwork in a remote team, project managers can create a team culture that values and supports sustainable performance, well-being, and work-life balance. When team members feel supported, empowered, and encouraged to prioritize their health and well-being, they are more likely to be engaged, productive, and committed to their work and their team, and to contribute to a positive and thriving work environment.

So if you're a remote project manager, make recognizing and addressing signs of burnout and overwork a top priority. Be aware of and attuned to the physical, emotional, behavioral, cognitive, and work-related symptoms of burnout and overwork, and take proactive and supportive steps to prevent, mitigate, and address these issues. Use tools and techniques such as employee well-being and engagement surveys, project management and time tracking tools, mental health and well-being resources and support, sustainable work habits and boundaries, and a culture of open communication and psychological safety. By effectively recognizing and addressing signs of burnout and overwork in your remote team, you'll be well-equipped to lead a team that is healthy, resilient, and thriving, and that can sustain high levels of performance and well-being over the long term.

Modeling Self-Care and Personal Development

As a remote project manager, modeling self-care and personal development is a powerful way to lead by example and create a team culture that values and supports well-being, growth, and balance. Self-care refers to the practices and activities that individuals engage in to maintain and improve their physical, emotional, and mental health, while personal development refers to the ongoing process of learning, growing, and improving oneself personally and professionally. When project managers prioritize and model self-care and personal development, they not only benefit their own well-being and effectiveness, but also inspire and empower their team members to do the same.

In a remote work environment, modeling self-care and personal development can be particularly important, as team members may face unique challenges and stressors related to isolation, work-life balance, and lack of in-person support and connection. By demonstrating and promoting healthy habits, boundaries, and growth mindset, project managers can create a positive and supportive remote work culture that enables team members to thrive and bring their best selves to their work and their team.

Here are some key strategies for modeling self-care and personal development as a remote project manager:

1. **Prioritize and communicate self-care practices**
   - Identify and prioritize the self-care practices that are most important and effective for you, such as exercise, meditation, hobbies, or social connection, and make time for them in your daily or weekly routine
   - Communicate and share your self-care practices with your team, and explain how they benefit your well-being, productivity, and leadership, and encourage team members to identify and prioritize their own self-care practices
   - Model and reinforce the value and importance of self-care by taking regular breaks, respecting work-life boundaries, and avoiding overwork or burnout, and by supporting and encouraging team members to do the same

2. **Engage in and share personal development activities**
   - Identify and pursue personal development activities that align with your goals, interests, and growth areas, such as learning a new skill, reading a book, attending a workshop, or seeking feedback or mentorship
   - Share your personal development activities and learnings with your team, and explain how they contribute to your growth, effectiveness, and leadership, and encourage team members to identify and pursue their own personal development activities
   - Create opportunities for team members to engage in and share personal development activities, such as through learning and development programs, peer coaching, or knowledge-sharing sessions, and celebrate and recognize their growth and achievements

3. **Foster a growth mindset and learning culture**
   - Cultivate and model a growth mindset, which is the belief that one's abilities and intelligence can be developed through effort, learning, and perseverance, and that challenges and failures are opportunities for growth and improvement
   - Encourage and support a learning culture within your team, where experimentation, risk-taking, and continuous improvement are valued and celebrated, and where feedback, collaboration, and knowledge-sharing are regular practices
   - Provide resources and opportunities for team members to develop their skills, knowledge, and capabilities, such as through training, mentoring, or stretch assignments, and support and encourage their professional development and career growth

4. **Practice and promote self-reflection and self-awareness**
   - Engage in regular self-reflection and self-awareness practices, such as journaling, feedback-seeking, or personality assessments, to gain insights into your strengths, weaknesses, values, and behaviors, and to identify areas for growth and improvement
   - Share your self-reflection insights and learnings with your team, and explain how they inform your leadership and decision-making, and encourage team members to engage in their own self-reflection and self-awareness practices

- Create a team culture that values and supports self-reflection and self-awareness, such as through regular check-ins, retrospectives, or 360-degree feedback processes, and that encourages openness, vulnerability, and personal growth

5. **Communicate and reinforce the importance of well-being and development**
   - Regularly communicate and reinforce the importance and benefits of self-care and personal development to your team and stakeholders, and explain how they contribute to individual and team performance, engagement, and well-being
   - Advocate for and implement policies, practices, and resources that support self-care and personal development, such as flexible work arrangements, wellness programs, or learning and development budgets, and ensure that they are accessible and inclusive for all team members
   - Celebrate and recognize team members who demonstrate a commitment to self-care and personal development, and who inspire and support others to do the same, and create a team culture that values and rewards well-being and growth

Modeling self-care and personal development as a remote project manager requires intentionality, consistency, and authenticity. It involves prioritizing and communicating self-care practices, engaging in and sharing personal development activities, fostering a growth mindset and learning culture, practicing and promoting self-reflection and self-awareness, and communicating and reinforcing the importance of well-being and development.

To effectively model self-care and personal development, remote project managers can use a variety of tools and techniques, such as:

- Using self-care and well-being apps, such as Calm, Headspace, or Fitbit, to track and prioritize self-care practices and habits, and to share progress and insights with the team
- Leveraging personal development and learning platforms, such as Coursera, Udemy, or TED, to access and pursue personal development activities and resources, and to share learnings and recommendations with the team
- Facilitating team-building and development activities, such as book clubs, skill-sharing sessions, or hackathons, to foster a growth mindset and learning culture, and to create opportunities for team members to learn and grow together
- Conducting regular self-reflection and feedback sessions, such as through journaling prompts, 360-degree feedback surveys, or one-on-one check-ins, to gain insights and identify areas for growth and improvement, and to model vulnerability and openness with the team
- Communicating and reinforcing the importance of self-care and personal development through team meetings, newsletters, or social media, and by advocating for and implementing policies and resources that support well-being and growth, such as wellness programs or learning and development budgets

By effectively modeling self-care and personal development, remote project managers can create a team culture that values and supports well-being, growth, and balance. When team members feel inspired, empowered, and supported to prioritize their own self-care and personal development, they are more likely to be engaged, motivated, and effective in their work and their team, and to contribute to a positive and thriving remote work environment.

So if you're a remote project manager, make modeling self-care and personal development a top priority. Prioritize and communicate self-care practices, engage in and share personal development activities, foster a growth mindset and learning culture, practice and promote self-reflection and self-awareness, and communicate and reinforce the importance of well-being and development. Use tools and techniques such as self-care and well-being apps, personal development and learning platforms, team-building and development activities, self-reflection and feedback sessions, and communication and advocacy strategies. By effectively modeling self-care and personal development, you'll be well-equipped to lead a remote team that is healthy, growing, and thriving, and that can sustain high levels of well-being and performance over the long term.

Conclusion

Congratulations! You've made it to the end of this comprehensive guide on how to become a successful remote project manager and lead virtual teams. Throughout this book, we've covered a wide range of topics and strategies, from the foundations of remote project management to the art of remote leadership, and everything in between.

Putting Your Skills into Practice
Now that you've gained a wealth of knowledge and insights on remote project management, it's time to put your skills into practice. Start by reviewing the key takeaways and action items from each chapter, and identify the areas where you can apply them to your own projects and teams.

Remember, remote project management is not a one-size-fits-all approach, and what works for one team or project may not work for another. Be adaptable, flexible, and open to experimenting with different tools, techniques, and strategies, and be willing to learn from your successes and failures.

Some practical steps you can take to put your skills into practice include:

- Conducting a remote project kickoff meeting with your team, using the guidelines and best practices from Chapter 4
- Implementing a communication plan and collaboration tools, based on the strategies from Chapter 6

- Facilitating a virtual team-building activity or social event, using the ideas from Chapter 8
- Providing feedback and coaching to a team member, using the techniques from Chapter 10
- Advocating for and implementing a work-life balance policy or wellness program, based on the principles from Chapter 13

Continual Learning and Improvement

As a remote project manager, your learning and growth journey never ends. The field of remote work and project management is constantly evolving, with new tools, trends, and best practices emerging all the time.

To stay ahead of the curve and continue to improve your skills and effectiveness, make a commitment to continual learning and improvement. This can involve:

- Attending webinars, conferences, or workshops on remote project management and leadership topics
- Reading books, articles, or blogs from thought leaders and practitioners in the field
- Joining online communities or forums, such as PMI, Scrum Alliance, or Remote PM, to network and share knowledge with other remote project managers
- Seeking feedback and mentorship from colleagues, stakeholders, or coaches, to gain insights and guidance on your strengths and areas for improvement
- Experimenting with new tools, techniques, or approaches, and measuring their impact and effectiveness on your projects and teams

- Reflecting on your own experiences and learnings, and documenting them in a journal, blog, or portfolio, to track your growth and share your insights with others

The Future of Remote Project Management

As we look to the future, it's clear that remote work and virtual teams are here to stay. The COVID-19 pandemic has accelerated the shift towards remote work, and many organizations are now embracing it as a long-term strategy for flexibility, cost savings, and talent access.

This means that the skills and strategies covered in this book will become even more critical and valuable for project managers in the years to come. To thrive in this new world of work, remote project managers will need to be adaptable, resilient, and innovative, and to continuously evolve their practices and mindsets to meet the changing needs and expectations of their teams and stakeholders.

Some key trends and opportunities that remote project managers should be aware of and prepare for include:

- The rise of asynchronous communication and collaboration, as teams become more distributed and global, and the need for real-time coordination decreases
- The increasing use of AI and automation tools, such as chatbots, predictive analytics, and robotic process automation, to streamline and optimize project management tasks and decision-making

- The growing importance of emotional intelligence, empathy, and cultural sensitivity, as remote teams become more diverse and inclusive, and the need for psychological safety and belonging increases
- The emergence of new project management methodologies and frameworks, such as agile, lean, and design thinking, that emphasize flexibility, iteration, and customer-centricity, and the need for remote project managers to adapt and integrate them into their practices

As a remote project manager, you have the opportunity and the responsibility to shape the future of work and to lead your teams and organizations towards success and impact. By continuously learning, improving, and innovating, and by leveraging the skills and strategies covered in this book, you can become a trailblazer and a change agent in the field of remote project management.

So go forth and put your skills into practice, embrace continual learning and improvement, and be prepared for the exciting and transformative future of remote project management. The world is your oyster, and the possibilities are endless. Good luck, and happy remote project managing!

www.ingramcontent.com/pod-product-compliance
Lightning Source LLC
Chambersburg PA
CBHW050050230526
45470CB00004B/1475